Flawed Strategy

Why Smart Leaders Make
Bad Decisions

BEATRICE HEUSER

Copyright © Beatrice Heuser 2025

The right of Beatrice Heuser to be identified as Author of this Work has been asserted in accordance with the UK Copyright, Designs and Patents Act 1988.

First published in 2025 by Polity Press

Polity Press
65 Bridge Street
Cambridge CB2 1UR, UK

Polity Press
111 River Street
Hoboken, NJ 07030, USA

All rights reserved. Except for the quotation of short passages for the purpose of criticism and review, no part of this publication may be reproduced, stored in a retrieval system or transmitted, in any form or by any means, electronic, mechanical, photocopying, recording or otherwise, without the prior permission of the publisher.

ISBN-13: 978-1-5095-6669-3
ISBN-13: 978-1-5095-6670-9 (pb)

A catalogue record for this book is available from the British Library.

Library of Congress Control Number: 2024937185

Typeset in 11 on 14 pt Warnock Pro
by Cheshire Typesetting Ltd, Cuddington, Cheshire
Printed and bound in Great Britain by CPI Group (UK) Ltd, Croydon

The publisher has used its best endeavours to ensure that the URLs for external websites referred to in this book are correct and active at the time of going to press. However, the publisher has no responsibility for the websites and can make no guarantee that a site will remain live or that the content is or will remain appropriate.

Every effort has been made to trace all copyright holders, but if any have been overlooked the publisher will be pleased to include any necessary credits in any subsequent reprint or edition.

For further information on Polity, visit our website:
politybooks.com

Contents

Acknowledgements	vi
Preface	vii
Introduction	1
1. The Rational/Irrational Actor Fallacy	9
2. Our Biases	52
3. Knowns and Unknowns (and How We Use Them)	108
4. Flaws and Quandaries of Strategy Making	132
Epilogue	166
Notes	170
Select Bibliography	190

Acknowledgements

This book was written for the Bundeswehr's General Staff College in Hamburg, the support of which I gratefully acknowledge. I had vital access to the University of Glasgow's library facilities, again something to be thankful for.

I want to express my profound gratitude for pertinent and highly useful feedback from several friends and colleagues, including especially Professors John Baylis, Samuël Kruizinga and Paul Schulte, who went through the whole text and pointed out many shortcomings. I also want to thank most warmly Dr Gill Bennett, Thomas Boehlke, Ambassador Dr Valerie Caton, Dr Jack Harding, David Harrison, Dr Rob Johnson, Professors Andreas Lutsch, David Yost and Eitan Shamir, Wg Cdr Harold Simpson and Dr Tim Sweijs, all of whom spotted flaws and pointed me to additional readings and considerations. All remaining mistakes are mine alone.

As always, I must thank my wonderful husband for his patience with me that has allowed us to clock up our thirtieth wedding anniversary as this book was being written. It is a never-ending mystery to me how he put up with me for so long, and my most ardent wish is that he will, illogically and irrationally, continue to do so.

Preface

This book is a reaction to the preponderance of theories in the discipline of International Relations (IR) that are generally taught with the claim to offer monocausal explanations of how international relations – the reality – work. That this approach dominates the teaching of IR has frustrated me greatly for years. Manuals tend to prescribe this theory-centric approach: select a theory, write a chapter or more just about theory, write another chapter about methodology (most of which states the all too obvious),[1] then take two or three case studies, see if they fit the theory, thus verify or falsify it, adapt it to fit the cases or discard it. This is usually formulated in terms of an 'independent variable' (whenever A) and a 'dependent variable' (then B), as one might in the natural sciences, for example with temperature and the volume occupied by gases. The original research on the case studies often constitutes a mere third of the work, sandwiched in between extensive discussions of theory of the sort that would have delighted medieval theologians. I see a glimmer of hope when students are encouraged to mix methodologies of research, or even test more than one theory against a case study. They are still taught, however, to select a couple of theories at most so that the result still looks viii Preface

reductionist. Students are shoehorned into this methodological approach, whether it is appropriate or not. Non-specialists will review their work – whether these are second or third examiners or annual reviewers of PhD students' work – looking out for this methodology if they are unfamiliar with the contents. If the standard procedure of theory – the identification of an 'independent variable' and a 'dependent variable' – is not applied, they will then claim that the methodology is deficient.

But this monocausal methodology rarely if ever fits Strategic Studies or the analysis of an adversary's intentions. Students of war and strategy have, since Carl von Clausewitz, recognized the interplay of *interdependent* variables in wars and tense relations between inimical parties, most famously in the Clausewitzian trinity of the passions, chance and deliberate policy.[2] He and other authors identified many other variables besides. I, for one, have yet to find a variable that is truly independent in the context of war and strategy. Even artillery trajectories depend not on just one variable but on several: gravity, weight and speed. The imposition of the methodology described above is thus thoroughly confusing.

On another point, hardly a conference with practitioners goes by, nor a seminar teaching undergraduates, Master's students or military officers at any level – including generals and admirals – without somebody raising the question of whether we are dealing with 'rational' adversaries. Depending on the answer to this, they will speculate as to whether certain strategic measures would 'make sense' when dealing with an 'irrational' adversary. What is meant by 'rational' in IR theory is whether, within the narrowly defined parameters of a theory, an actor is behaving as expected. It is always assumed, of course, that 'we' are 'rational'. In other words, we endeavour to argue and write in a scholarly and thus rational way, using the same reasoning throughout (I guess that is what is meant by 'rigorous', another term often used in that context). Given the specialization of subjects in universities, however, at a guess

Preface

ix

90 per cent of the students or practitioners I come across have not encountered critiques of rational choice theory, let alone studied psychology. As a result, one is forced to go over this argument every time. This book is designed to help do so.

The same applies to biases – irrational approaches – that we have ourselves. Such biases are studied and highlighted by psychologists, and several have also been discovered by historians in their specific historical studies, even if they have never read psychology.[3] But biases do not feature much in the most important classic IR theories: realism, liberalism or liberal institutionalism, Marxism and, above all, rational choice theory. Even idealism, constructivism and critical theory assume a conscious choice of positions, rather than one generated by unconscious biases.[4] The discussion of such biases will therefore form an important part of the analysis that follows.

While whether we can work out what adversaries think and how they might react to what we do, and whether we ourselves are being irrational, has practical implications, theoreticians in the field of IR in recent times seem largely to have lost interest in practical implications. Instead, most seem entirely focused on the *Glasperlenspiel* (Hermann Hesse), the purely academic activity of playing with theories, detached from reality, as though theories were what mattered, not whether one can give sound advice to practitioners.

It should be said that this book is not the only one dealing with biases in strategic analysis. It is much to the US Marine Corps War College's credit that it has included appendices in its *Strategy Primer* of 2021 – a manual giving guidance on how to formulate good strategy – that deal with (often false or misguiding) assumptions and biases.[5] Sir David Omand, who spent most of his career in British intelligence, rising to head of the Government Communications Headquarters, has also dealt with such biases in his fascinating book on *How Spies Think*.[6] In both cases, the hope is that by identifying biases, one might fight them, but it is clear that neither book is written with the hope of eradicating this human weakness. Nor can the current book present the reader with a recipe to avoid *all* errors of analysis. But it may go some way to deepening our understanding of why seemingly intelligent and well-informed leaders continue to make poor strategic decisions with outcomes that are at best ill-judged but with minimal repercussions and, at worst, will negatively impact the course of history and people's lives.

Introduction

War, just like a non-violent conflict that may turn into armed conflict, is a dialectic activity – between at least two parties. Each side tries, through a strategy of its own, to force the enemy to do its will, as Carl von Clausewitz put it. The point *may* come where the enemy is completely disarmed and has no choice other than to do our will. Short of such a situation, however, each side tries to influence the behaviour of the other until the other gives up, gives in, surrenders, agrees to an armistice or to some other form of compromise. Influencing the other side through strategy – the use of force and/or of non-violent means – assumes an action–reaction mechanism, in which we can somehow trigger reactions advantageous to us on the part of the enemy and avoid reactions that will be detrimental, perhaps even devastating, for us. Especially when confronted with an adversary armed with nuclear weapons, but not only then, strategy making is a precarious balancing act in which it is vital to anticipate an adversary's reactions to one's every move, both in times of crisis and actual war. In war, and to manage difficult relationships that could lead to war, we therefore need to understand what our adversaries think, want and do. We need to understand their strategies and their

Introduction

strategic reasoning. It is no good just to know what aims *we* have in mind, even if we have very smart minds. That is likely to lead to flawed strategy, bad decision making on the part of leaders that, at times, has serious domestic and international consequences.

Dealing with a nuclear-armed adversary is an extreme case, of course. Even armed conflict is extreme. Much more frequent are situations in international relations in which national leaders or representatives of a government or an international organization are dealing with one another in non-violent ways, negotiating over issues that might well lead to outcomes of mutual benefits, to 'win–win' situations, rather than ones in which one side imposes its will upon the other. But there, too, when differing approaches and attitudes meet, 'the trick' (as British diplomat Baroness Neville-Jones calls it) is to see where adversaries are coming from, and how they think and why.

The first step to understanding an adversary is usually to put ourselves in their shoes, to empathize, to imagine how we would think and do in their place. Often enough, however, adversaries do not oblige us by thinking or behaving as we would, leading to great puzzlement on our side. As in the fairy tale Cinderella, we might have to chop off toes or heels, that is, our own preconceptions and assumptions, for the shoe to fit.

Under the influence of economists who have exerted a strong influence on Strategic Studies ever since we entered the nuclear age, most literature on strategy still assumes 'rational actors' on both sides of a conflict. Strategic Studies is usually seen as a sub-discipline of the study of the interaction of governments. For that is the essence of the discipline we call International Relations (IR), even though it is rarely about the relations between nations unless they are engaged in 'total' wars with one another where the whole of the nation is mobilized. Key IR theories, especially those derived directly from game theories, assume that decision making is a predictable game. Economists assume that there is a *Homo economicus*

Introduction

who will choose which espresso machine he will buy, or which university to apply to, by doing extensive market research, his decision guided only by applying criteria such as cost, customer satisfaction feedback on the machine, or the university's standing in league tables. Key IR theories assume that similar cost–benefit criteria are applied when decision makers ponder whether to invade another country or to use nuclear weapons. Strategic concepts such as deterrence, dissuasion, coercion, compulsion or the whole notion of crisis management are built on the assumption that one is playing a game of chess or a similar highly rule-bound game – hence the importance of game theory, imported from economics – in which moves are expected to produce rational, calculable responses. In reality, such theories and concepts are built on sand: they are profoundly challenged by adversaries holding fundamental beliefs which we do not share, not to mention the many considerations they may have that we have not thought of.[1] Moreover, as we shall see in the following chapters, the processes of arriving at decisions collectively are in themselves obstacles to the pursuit of a single logic, or rational reasoning.

By contrast, historians exposed to IR theories are usually astounded by the claim that these theories can provide monocausal explanations.[2] Historians since Thucydides have been aware that strategic decisions are not made based on a single issue. Strategy making is all about prioritization, weighing expected consequences and choosing what one thinks might be the lesser evil. Moreover, historians are all too aware that, of course, emotions and notions of pride and reputation colour and distort decision makers' thinking. Already, Thucydides evoked 'fear, honour and interest' as the *three* great factors motivating humans to go to war. Therefore, what outsiders might see as rational cost–benefit calculations are so often squeezed out by blind fury, fear and interests, clearly not those of the nation as a whole.[3] This lesson was learned a long time ago by those who read Ivan Bloch's work written on the eve of

4   Introduction

the First World War that explained how utterly irrational and self-destructive it would be for the prosperous, commercially interconnected European states to go to war with one another,[4] or Norman Angell's argument that it was a 'great illusion' to think that any nation could benefit truly from such a war.[5]

Diplomatic historians – historians burrowing deep into government archives, often with a view to understanding the origins of a particular war or the obstacles to making peace – have long been aware that decisions are made at the highest level with incomplete knowledge about what an adversary has in terms of means, what he intends to do or what the comparative costs and benefits would be to one's own side if one tried to stop his expansionism now or later. The very title of a recent bestseller on the origins of the First World War, *The Sleepwalkers*,[6] sums this up neatly. And the debate about whether Britain and France would have been better off if they had refused Hitler's demand for the Sudetenland to be ceded to neighbouring Germany by Czechoslovakia in late 1938, rather than declaring war on Germany a year later when Hitler invaded Poland after the *Wehrmacht* had occupied the rest of Czechoslovakia and turned its east into a 'protectorate', is continuing.[7]

Box 0.1: The Eve of the Second World War

After the First World War, a democratic Germany had gradually gained the confidence of its neighbours until the economic crisis following the Wall Street Crash of 1929 led to the rise of the extreme left and right. Hitler, heading the racist National Socialist ('Nazi') Party, came to power in Germany in 1933. While successive French governments were wary, British governments continued to show goodwill towards Germany, hoping that condoning Hitler's piecemeal dismantlement of Germany's limitations imposed by the post-First World War peace treaty signed at Versailles would appease him.

Introduction

In 1936, Germany annexed the Rhineland – according to the Versailles Treaty, this was to remain demilitarized – and then, in 1938, Austria – a separate state. Hitler then demanded that Czechoslovakia cede the Sudetenland to Germany, a mountainous region along the Czech–German border, in part populated by German speakers of Austrian culture. The British Prime Minister Sir Neville Chamberlain and, persuaded by him, the French head of government Edouard Daladier, at a conference in Munich in September 1938 pressed the Czech President Edvard Beneš to comply with Hitler's demands.

Hitler promised that this was his last territorial demand, but only weeks later he ordered plans to be drawn up to 'finish off' the rest of Czechoslovakia. In March 1939, these orders were carried out; the *Wehrmacht* invaded Czechoslovakia, which was now unable to put up a proper defence against the superior force descending from the western and northern heights of the Sudetenland. This finally persuaded Chamberlain and Daladier to stop appeasement and instead to draw a red line: if Germany now attacked Poland, its next victim, as German propaganda indicated, Britain and France would declare war on Germany. Hitler did not believe they would, proceeded to attack Poland on 1 September 1939 and was surprised when the British and French declarations of war were duly made.

Then psychologists, most prominently the Nobel prize-winning Daniel Kahneman, articulated their astonishment at the assumptions underlying rational actor theory or rational choice theory (these terms are used synonymously in the following).[8] They have shown that, however smart we are, none of us are fully 'rational actors' as we are subject to a wide range of biases affecting our – and governments' – interpretations of the world and our behaviour.[9] As a consequence, smart leaders and their representatives sometimes make bad decisions.

Economists' classical assumptions that all the actors in economists' theories are rational have since been questioned

6 Introduction

fundamentally, and a rich debate has ensued between economists and psychologists, especially since the 1990s.[10] Under pressure from this critique, even some scholars in IR have questioned the premises of much of their own discipline, especially the research focused on how to influence an adversary. For that assumes that this is predictable and calculable, sometimes even that we do not need to know more about the particularities of adversaries and can guess how they will react simply by imagining how we would react ourselves.

More recently still, a number of studies of deterrent statements and ultimatums have found that deterrence does not always work as intended, and that there are multiple causes for this, making the reaction to an act or posture designed to deter difficult to predict.[11] Given that theories around deterrence, coercion and compellence occupy such an important place in Strategic Studies, this deals potentially lethal blows to the clay feet of 'deterrence theory', a colossus among IR theories.[12] The variety of possible reactions to deterrence in a non-nuclear context in what we might call a 'post-rationalist approach' to deterrence theory is the discussion of Lawrence Freedman – himself one of the key contributors to the literature on deterrence – of possible deterrent steps and possible reactions on the part of regional players in the Hamas–Israel War that started on 7 October 2023.[13] He argued that in this complex context, neat theories of deterrence may not work according to the textbooks. It is uncertain what strategic moves will 'work' to pacify the region: they might have one, or the opposite, effect.[14] Scepticism concerning our ability to devise sure-fire strategies that will predictably compel our adversaries to behave in the way we want them to is thus in order.

In the following chapters, the realization that decision making is riddled with biases and irrational choices will be applied to analysis and decision making in the context of crises, when there is a danger of war or when one is actually at war.

Introduction

Chapter 1 is a further assault on the concept of the 'rational actor', using historical examples to illustrate how problematic it is. If this concept collapses, then with it should any notion that we can carefully control and calibrate strategies towards adversaries in a conflictual context. Indeed, we should let go of the notion that the way we think and act is the gold standard of 'rationality', and that our adversaries think like us and will respond to moves we make the way we would if we were standing in their place. Chapter 2 will turn to the many biases with which we, who like to think of ourselves as 'rational', interpret the actions of others, specifically in the context of conflictual international relations.

Chapter 3 will discuss problems we have with knowing what we need to know to make good decisions, and how to apply what we may know. Chapter 4 will discuss how policies are assumed to be arrived at, and how this often works in reality. It will shed light on the boundaries of choices we can make in the light of our limited abilities to predict, let alone to weigh up, future outcomes.

Finally, in the epilogue, I close with a summary of widespread fallacies and biases which the student, the foreign and security-policy analyst, the diplomat, the strategy maker but also the journalist or indeed the thinking citizen should guard against.

* * *

There is a growing gulf between, on the one hand, the knowledge of academics working in the field of international history (especially twentieth-century international history) and the lessons that have been drawn by earlier generations from well-studied wars and crises and, on the other, what current practitioners and younger generations know about these events as they fade from living memory. Even students of International Relations – the discipline and especially its theories – may not have encountered these key wars and crises of the twentieth century if they have not taken a module on twentieth-century history. For non-specialists and for younger readers, therefore, textboxes such as Box 0.1 (p. 4) are included to summarize the historical context from which examples are drawn.

1

The Rational/Irrational Actor Fallacy

Historians have, at least since Thucydides, tried to explain decision making in war and peace in terms that would seem reasonable to their smart and discerning readers. This presumes a common logic and a common rationality guiding decisions to explain them in ways that make sense to the author and readers alike. Foreign Policy Analysis – now seen as an established toolbox meriting handbooks to accompany students through their modules on International Relations – generally assumes, not merely a *logic* common to humans even though it might be based on differing premises, beliefs, values and assumptions, but 'rational actors' on all sides.

The term 'rational actor' goes back a long way, at least to the father of economics, the great Glaswegian Adam Smith, who based his economic reasoning on the assumption that actors make choices based on cost–benefit analyses. As Herbert Simon, an early critic of the concept, noted, 'practically the whole of classic economic theory is constructed within the framework of [rational actor] theory.'[1] Nevertheless, it forms the basis of many contemporary domains which he tried to influence, including studies of information processing,

10 The Rational/Irrational Actor Fallacy

problem solving, decision making, artificial intelligence and theories of organization and complex systems.

In economics, rational actor or rational choice theory supposes that:

1. The individual is the basic agent in society.
2. Individual actors pursue consistent and enduring goals that reflect their self-interests.
3. The individual identifies one main goal, and then decisions are taken in pursuit of that goal.
4. In their decision making (or 'choices' made), actors possess all the information they need on available options, their costs, their benefits and the likely consequences of their choices. They will thus act in full knowledge of the causality and consequences of their choices.
5. If they have several options to choose from, they will choose that with the highest expected feasibility and utility in achieving their self-interested goals.[2]

If all these premises are true, therefore, the theory is that actors' choices can be predicted if one knows what choices are available to them.

Transposed to politics, and to the specific realm of International (or rather inter-governmental) Relations (IR), there are several problems with these assumptions.

1. There are few states where supreme decisions are made by just one individual. Even in many autocracies or monarchies, the chief decision maker is expected to listen to wise counsellors, and where these have power bases – running whole organizations or owning large territories or other assets – he or she can only get away with ignoring the latter's advice so many times before they become disaffected and may attempt to rebel against perceived tyranny. Government decision making is usually, at least to some degree, collective.

The Rational/Irrational Actor Fallacy

2 Accordingly, the reasoning behind decisions tends to be influenced by multiple goals and interests, and veers away to a lesser or greater degree from the purely consistent and logical pursuit of one clearly identified goal and towards compromises. Moreover, not all actors act exclusively out of sheer self-interest.

3 As discussed further below, individuals and groups involved in decision making have multiple goals which might fluctuate in importance, are interrelated or interdependent.

4 Then, as noted in the introduction, in real-live situations decision makers rarely if ever have all the information they need to make the best choices in full cognizance of their consequences.

5 Given the multiplicity of goals and the limitations on means available to pursue them, plus speculations about the reactions of an adversary, and taking into account public opinion, allies and partners, and other such factors, the choices made are not necessarily those with highest utility in a purely technical sense, as the political implications of such choices may run counter to what is to be achieved. Just think of why no nuclear power, despite being involved in wars, has used nuclear weapons in war since 1945, even though physically they might have resolved many an operational problem quite decisively.

The very assumption that all actors would take decisions in predictable ways, based on prioritizing the same values, is misleading. Even when it comes to defining self-interest, opinions on what that might be can diverge. As political scientist William Riker put it, 'what people want to do varies widely, ranging from private advantage, power over others, or greed for wealth, to the intention of helping others even to the extreme of wishing to sacrifice one's own life . . . man is not always concerned with maximising income . . .'.[3] Just think of the quest for 'power', assumed by so much political theory

12 The Rational/Irrational Actor Fallacy

to be at the heart of politics. Power to do what? To achieve some sort of selfish gratification in being able to dominate others? Or to get good things done, overriding the inertia of bureaucracy? Out of blind devotion to a particular cause? To impose religious rules on secular societies, or to overcome selfish obstacles on the part of other actors to policies that would be in the objective interests of the polity as a whole (as, for example, to impose a speed limit of 130 km per hour on all German motorways)? Such devotion can be quite selfless and altruistic – from risking jail in protest against a tyrannical regime to becoming suicide bombers for a particular cause. To sum up, rational actor theory 'does not apply consistently enough once we enter the realm of the political', as Riker's colleague Kristen Monroe put it.[4]

Nor can one always identify a single goal or isolate a single issue on which an adversary decides. Strategy making is about prioritizing some goals over others in a world where even the world's most powerful country, the United States, has limited means. But this does not mean that the other goals – or problems that have to be addressed – disappear. A balance has to be found in meeting or deterring threats from different directions, or warding off military threats while tackling others that will devour huge parts of a state's income. In today's Europe, dealing with the budget deficit left by tackling the Covid-19 pandemic and investing in cleaner sources of energy to mitigate climate change have to be balanced against deterring further Russian expansionism and helping Ukraine defend against the Russian invasion, and coping with the influx of refugees from various parts of the world afflicted by war and other crises. Decisions made on any one of these affect what decisions can be made on the others.

In short, we do indeed find that the criteria for working out what an adversary wants cannot simply be those developed for economics, nor even for the parts of political science that deal with voters' behaviour. We should experiment with other

The Rational/Irrational Actor Fallacy

approaches while steering clear of further fallacies with their own distinctive roots.

Rationality versus logic

Some political scientists have homed in on the fundamental differences between the basic values and ethical assumptions of different cultures which they think reduce the utility of rational actor theory, once we enter the realm of IR. Roxanne has studied fundamentalist Islam as an example, the adherents of which act not in self-interest but to fulfil what they believe to be God's will. According to some readings, the Koran does not even guarantee a heavenly reward in return for good deeds (including martyrdom), but any reward remains subject to God's will.[5]

Differing basic beliefs, even ones seen as quite irrational by others, can nevertheless help us identify a regime's policies, as long as those holding them are acting *logically and coherently*, given those beliefs. The issue is not whether actors have beliefs which we regard as irrational – others today may and people in the future most likely will find some or all of *our* beliefs quite irrational. The question is whether one's adversary (or indeed an ally or other government) is acting *logically and coherently* on the basis of their beliefs, whatever they are, whether or not we find them 'rational'. As psychologists have realized, there can be logic in 'ordinary' madness. If it is an accepted premise in a particular culture that one must do everything to increase one's nation's standing in the world, then it would be *logical* for leaders of a nation with this culture to go to war if that is seen as increasing its standing. This might include risking the nation's total destruction (logically, if the nation's 'standing' in the world is seen as an *absolute* value that must be striven for uncompromisingly). In *Mein Kampf*, Hitler wrote, 'Germany will either be a world power or not at all' (the German *'gar*

14 The Rational/Irrational Actor Fallacy

nicht sein' having the implication of 'ceasing to exist').[6] This latter outcome would be *irrational* to risk for anybody regarding a nation's standing only as a *relative* value, with the survival of the nation a greater value. Even in the (for Hitler, unacceptable) position of a minor power, survival would hold out future possibilities of grandeur, whereas total destruction would not. The case of Hitler is thus evidence that ideology- or religion-driven governments and other actors do not always make the survival of their state or nation the highest priority (which is how Mearsheimer and Rosato define 'rationality', and which they claim applies universally to government decision making[7]). The fear of a fate worse than death – perceived as such in terms of values, or truly existent in the form of unspeakably inhumane treatment and living conditions in labour camps – might after all drive a regime to risk its own country's total destruction.[8]

Similarly, it may have been incompatible with British 'common sense' that Yugoslav President Slobodan Milošević in 1998–9 endeavoured to expel or displace 90 per cent of the population of Kosovo in an attempt to thwart the Kosovar Albanian independence movement, but it had a certain logic within his Serb nationalist worldview. Given his total dedication to the grandeur of Serbia, which in his mind could only be upheld if it did not lose control of Kosovo, the 'cradle' of Serb civilization for a Kosovar Albanian independence movement, the large-scale 'ethnic cleansing' of the Kosovar Albanians had an inherent logic. To outsiders, the premises made no sense, and his behaviour was deemed irrational, given the huge cost to Serbia in the form of political isolation, sanctions and then NATO bombardment.

The Rational/Irrational Actor Fallacy

Box 1.1: The Kosovo Crisis, 1998–9

Kosovo was a state of the Serb-dominated Federation of Yugoslavia that was named after the battlefield where the collective myth of Serb identity was forged in 1389 in an epic defeat of self-sacrificing Serbs by an attacking Muslim Ottoman host. Like Kiev in Ukraine, as the 'cradle' of Russian civilization, Kosovo, with its old monasteries and its battlefield that served to forge Serb national identity, came to occupy a particular emotional place in the Serb collective mentality.

In the twentieth century, however, ethnic Albanian Muslims gradually became the majority population in Kosovo due to their high birth rates, while the Serbs, still de facto the ruling elite, became a minority. Kosovar Albanians repeatedly staged protests against this distribution of power, and by the end of the 1990s they had formed paramilitary groups willing to use violence to follow the path of other parts of Yugoslavia that in the 1990s had achieved independence: Slovenia, Croatia and Bosnia-Herzegovina. By 1998–9, a Kosovo dominated by the Serbs seemed to Yugoslav President Slobodan Milošević, a Serb, the only remaining way to keep Serb-dominated Yugoslavia alive, which by then consisted only of Serbia, Kosovo and two other entities. Attacks and selective killings of Kosovar Albanians perpetrated by Serb police and military forces, initially just targeting guerrilla groups and their supporters, began in 1998. Then it escalated in March 1999 to large-scale 'ethnic cleansing', the Serb-organized movement of well over a million Kosovar Albanians away from certain areas within Kosovo.

Afraid that this would turn into genocide and would lead to massacres similar to those that had taken place only a few years before in Bosnia-Herzegovina (culminating in the Srebrenica Massacre of 1995), governments of NATO member-states felt the strong moral pressure to act preventively. No UN Security Council resolution came forth to back this as Russia, a veto power of the Council, protected Milošević, the rest of Yugoslavia having effectively become Moscow's client state. Hesitantly, scarred by the guilt of non-intervention in the Rwandan genocide of 1994 and the non-prevention of the Srebrenica massacre, in 1999 the governments of NATO member-states eventually agreed, first to threaten and, if Milošević persisted with his operations in Kosovo, to launch a bombing campaign against Milošević's capital, Belgrade, to stop them. Without a United Nations (UN) mandate, this intervention was legally questionable, but it was felt to be legitimate as it aimed to prevent a humanitarian catastrophe. It deeply alienated Russia, which until that point had cooperated fairly constructively with the western members of the UN Security Council, and indeed with NATO.

It is difficult to prove that events that were prevented would otherwise have taken place. But given Milošević's previous record of ordering and/or condoning the horrendous treatment of non-Serb populations in Bosnia, similar intentions on his part were assumed.

Sometimes actors, even smart actors, may act quite logically and coherently on their beliefs, however irrational these beliefs may seem to us. At other times, such coherence breaks down, as the beliefs and values of an individual or a culture rarely constitute a logically coherent whole, regardless of whether in themselves they are rational. Individual beliefs may contradict one another, values one holds might clash, especially for those who do not think through their own beliefs and values logically. This is why one should not presume to be dealing with coherent 'belief systems' but with 'belief clusters', which may contain many contradictory beliefs.[9] Individuals might thus prioritize one value or belief on one day but be more strongly influenced by another value or belief on another. For example, Christianity as a whole never quite settled the question of whether killing can be entirely exculpated in the context of a just war: from pagan times, it inherited the postulate that

The Rational/Irrational Actor Fallacy 17

the fighter for a just cause must not have a lust for revenge, let alone for killing itself, nor feel hatred – a mental disposition which, in the midst of slashing swords or flying bullets, presumably is quite hard to achieve. In the Middle Ages, even those fighting for a just cause on the orders of their lords (as the legitimate authority) had to do penance and abstain from communion for a certain length of time after such a campaign. Only in Western Christendom's Crusades was the act of killing an enemy combatant seen as completely without sin[10]; the Greek Orthodox Church never agreed that a war could be holy in any way.[11] To this day, some branches of Christianity, such as Quakers and Anabaptists, are of course pacifist, that is, they reject war for any reason, even self-defence.

Values and beliefs rarely constitute a coherent whole because they tend to be accumulated over generations under different regimes with differing ideologies. France's presidency under the present Fifth Republic with state power concentrated greatly in the hands of the president can be seen as rooted in the monarchical tradition of absolutism, while Britain's prime ministers, in the system of cabinet rule, stand in the tradition of the constitutional monarchy that Britain became in the late seventeenth century. On a more banal level of social mores, the egalitarian French are less likely to be on first-name terms than Americans and Britons, and that despite the British class system that is still reflected in knighthoods and peerages at the House of Lords. In theory, as in France, Germany recognizes no nobility; in practice, however, Germans can have titles like 'Countess', 'Duke' or 'Prince' integrated into their names when printed in their passports. Several countries, among them Germany, have constitutions stipulating equality between men and women, yet impose military service only on men. The Federal Republic of Germany also initially continued to carry legislation inherited from the Nazis. For example, homosexuality that had been criminalized only under National Socialist rule in 1935 continued to be so until 1994. Whether cultures

18   The Rational/Irrational Actor Fallacy

and mentalities change slowly, or fast after a strategic shock, traces of earlier customs, beliefs and values often survive reforms and revolutions.

Playing on another's values

Why do beliefs and whether they are applied logically and consistently matter? Discovering what others – especially leaders of states, polities or other organized groups – hold dear gives more anticipatory value to analysing their postures and plans than simply projecting our own thinking onto them. It allows us to make *educated* guesses as to what governments of other states or leaders of important non-state entities are up to, are planning or how they are likely to behave and react. Are they favouring peaceful cohabitation, are they engaged in a prolonged vendetta with one or more neighbours, or are they even set on a path of expansionism? We may find that they – or different parts of one government – are doing several things at the same time, perhaps things that may seem to us or objectively to be mutually contradictory. But such actions, whether logically coherent or not, are still more predictable if we understand others' mindsets.

In the context of war and peace, such analyses may even help a government play on what their adversaries value, in propaganda, or in making concessions on certain points to obtain cooperation in return. Alexander III ('the Great') of Macedon won over Persian and Egyptian hearts and minds when conquering these countries by embracing local rituals and culture. In Persia, he adopted the dress style of royalty and embraced the custom of proskynesis in which Persians bowed or knelt down in front of their rulers, which revolted his Macedonian and Greek companions but clearly helped him assert his authority among the Persians. He appealed to Egyptian culture by performing traditional Egyptian rituals and presenting himself as the son of the local deity Ammon,

The Rational/Irrational Actor Fallacy   19

again fitting in with the customs and traditions of the local population. This was a smart use of soft power.

By contrast, the Egyptian regent Pothinus spectacularly misjudged the Roman mentality in general and Caesar's in particular when murdering Caesar's rival, Pompey, who had sought refuge in Egypt, and then presenting Caesar with Pompey's head. Caesar saw this as a dishonourable way to defeat his former friend-turned-rival Pompey whom he had encountered in successive battles and pursued to Egypt. Even if it cost far more in lives and treasure, Caesar wanted to defeat Pompey in battle, not have him assassinated.

An admirable example of successfully playing on an adversary's beliefs and mentality can be found in the European 'Dark Ages'. When the Roman Empire crumbled in Gaul and civilians no longer had the protection of the legions of Rome to fend off Germanic onslaughts, the bishops of various cities of the provinces assumed the responsibility for protecting these. Often without any regular armed forces and with poorly organized militias, they had to resort to other means of dealing with the invading hordes of pagans whose booty raids were the chief threat to their cities. When they saw that the Germanic chiefs wanted more prestige for themselves and respect from their followers, they cleverly created a (non-violent) win–win strategy by suggesting they convert to Christianity. In the Jewish tradition, Christianity elevated tribal chiefs to be kings, chosen by God, anointed by priests, blessed and protected by a sacrament that made it taboo to challenge, let alone kill, them. Christianization became an important strategic tool, helping integrate barbarian invaders peacefully with the local populations, establishing rules of conduct (such as not to loot, rape and kill) and harnessing the leaders to a programme of creating law and order in return for putting them at the top of the secular hierarchy, endowed with a religious aura they had previously lacked. Several key bishops and other church leaders thus persuaded the tribal leaders to stop attacking

20 The Rational/Irrational Actor Fallacy

and pillaging the towns and countryside of the former Roman Empire. These smart clergymen thus turned Germanic poachers into gamekeepers: only a few generations later, the settled Germanic warriors would defend Gaul against Arab attacks.

Similarly, a little later, when Goths, Bulgars, Slavs and Arabs lusted after the wealth of Constantinople, smart Byzantine emperors also tried non-violent strategic solutions. Simply handing them large presents of money, however, often gave them a taste for more, so that proved sub-optimal. It was found to be more constructive to marry them to Byzantine princesses who would move to their new realms, accompanied by a cultural SWAT team of theologians and artisans, scholars and artists who would use the soft power of superior Byzantine culture to win over the locals. Emperors would bestow ranks of junior emperors (*caesar*, which became *tsar*) upon their sons-in-law and bring them into the imperial family, giving them imperial prestige (in addition to the mystique of Christian kingship). Several barbarian chiefs, such as Bulgar *knyaz* Boris I, were content with this alternative to assailing Constantinople for booty and slaves; others, such as the West Roman Emperor Otto I and his descendants, were turned from competitors into allies. Dynastic marriages were thus used as a tool of strategy.[12]

Common interests were served also by dictators who coalesced to keep each other's backs free as they embarked on expansionist wars, famously, of course, the regimes of fascist Italy, Nazi Germany and militaristic Japan in the 1930s. Understanding what the other wanted, they could de-conflict their plans and act in mutual support. Moreover, antagonists may temporarily collude to defeat a common enemy. Hitler's ideology pitted him strategically against communism, and he regarded Slavs as *Untermenschen* who should relinquish their fertile lands to Aryan farmers. Nor was Soviet communism more favourably inclined towards National Socialism, the fiercest enemy of communism in the 1930s, when many of the

The Rational/Irrational Actor Fallacy 21

early inmates of Hitler's concentration camps were German communists. Both Hitler and Stalin were keen to buy time, however, and they both coveted a part of Poland which Prussia and Russia respectively had occupied before the First World War. Thus in August 1939 they signed a pact of non-aggression, containing a secret appendix on the joint annexation of Poland.

Communism ultimately had in common with the western countries the assumption that the interests of humanity as a whole must be served. While Stalin, Mao and Pol Pot as communist leaders were quite willing to accept and indeed cause the deaths of millions – including their own citizens – for the supposed greater good of the surviving majority, other communist leaders were not. The USSR's governments of the late 1960s and the following decades were sufficiently awed by the danger of nuclear war to come to agreements on nuclear arms control with the United States.

The current Russian and Chinese regimes do not share our concern for *individual* human rights much more than did the more benign of the Soviet leaders. They promote their own approach internationally as a counter-model to the values of the West: what they see as the interests of society as a whole are held above the interests of minorities, whom they are willing to sacrifice. The clumsy title of Putin's decree of 9 November 2022, 'On approving the foundations of the state policy for preserving and strengthening traditional Russian spiritual and moral values', nicely sums up this strategic priority.[13]

In short, *beliefs* (e.g., the earth being flat) or *values* (e.g., valuing unquestioning obedience until death in all circumstances, *Kadavergehorsam*) that differ from ours, be they objectively irrational or merely different, should not bar us from making educated guesses as to how their holders will apply them in international relations, if individuals or collectives act on them *logically* and *coherently*. We should therefore ask whether actors act logically on their beliefs, rather than whether we find them irrational.

22   The Rational/Irrational Actor Fallacy

Don't judge decisions in hindsight alone

Once we have accepted that other states' leaders may truly hold and prioritize values we think irrational, there is a further case to be made for sometimes assuming *more* logic and coherence in their judgement than they are often given credit for. We can test this with regard to key leaders of the past (of any political hue) whose judgements have been dismissed as unreasonable in hindsight by historians. Any decision is based on what is known at the time and at best on predictions of the future that are necessarily limited. With hindsight, we may know that a decision was bad, plain wrong or had unintended consequences, but we may also be ignorant of what decision makers knew at the time, and thus of the logic on which this decision was based.

In 1950, early on in the Cold War, the US administration under President Harry S. Truman decided on a massive rearmament project. Critics of Truman, writing in particular in the 1970s against the backdrop of the catastrophic outcome of the Vietnam War, pointed to this decision – encapsulated in the US National Security Council's document NSC 68 – as the beginning of a foolish precipitation of America into a global fight against communism. Not only did NSC 68 kick off a build-up of American forces in Europe, which had been reduced very significantly after the end of the Second World War. It was also following Truman's lead that other equally worried parties to the North Atlantic Treaty, signed the previous year, agreed to underpin this alliance with an organization, the 'O' in NATO. Then, two years later, the other allies agreed at NATO's Lisbon Summit to increase their forces and, also at Lisbon, the allies decided on the first enlargement of NATO by admitting Greece and Turkey. Moreover, the question of how to harness West German manpower to the western defence effort was first tackled at the time, something that even France and other victims of

The Rational/Irrational Actor Fallacy 23

German aggression and occupation in the very recent past now thought reasonable.

While it is true that NSC 68 was drawn up *before* the invasion of South Korea by North Korea, American and other western intelligence reports in 1949–50 had already named this as a possible event. They sketched the possibility or even considerable likelihood that Moscow-directed communist forces were about to go on the offensive in several places along the periphery of the Soviet-dominated landmass from Germany and Iran to the Pacific region. It was thought that any one such move might be the first in a series, one of several conquests by 'salami' tactics. This emerged only when American archives were opened, giving researchers access to these intelligence reports. One can speculate as to whether NSC 68 and the rearmament scheme would have been adopted by the US administration if the Korean War had not confirmed at least one of these predictions. While no other aggressive moves were made by communist regimes immediately thereafter, Moscow may have renounced or put off earlier plans to put pressure on Iran or Berlin or Yugoslavia in the light of the forceful western reaction to the invasion of South Korea. Either way, the decision to adopt NSC 68 looks less foolish and more comprehensible in the light of the intelligence estimates of the time, documents that were not yet accessible to the scholars who initially denounced the foolhardiness of this great rearmament scheme.[14] In other words, what has been criticized as an unreasonable decision in hindsight (it *did* exacerbate East–West tensions) might look less so when the information available at the time of decision making has been reconstructed. A threat might have looked greater at the time, or leaders might have seen an opportunity for bettering their situation where in fact there was none.

There are other cases that in hindsight are clear and devastating mistakes of appreciation. Even in some of these, decision

24 The Rational/Irrational Actor Fallacy

makers were not outright foolish but did what they could with the information they had.

Monolithic actor fallacy

A government may be perceived as acting oddly, 'irrationally', if it is unreasonably presumed to be 'monolithic', with all its members and ministers acting coherently, in unison and in complete agreement. In reality, there is usually some internal consultation, debate and bargaining, and differences of opinion may well persist even if a firm position has been adopted. Subsequently, actors involved in the previous decision-making process may return to proposals that were not taken up, or to similar proposals, and as events unfold, they may find their position strengthened. Collective decisions often contain their own contradictions: the arguments against the decision may not go away but may be strengthened in a later round of decision making concerning the same adversary or a similar situation. Indeed, if the first decision is seen as having been mistaken, having led to unintended, negative consequences, then the arguments that went unheeded in it will gain in weight thereafter – and, with them, those who argued against the first decision. A case in point is that of the appeasement of Hitler. Those who had opposed it in Britain would come to power early on in the Second World War, and the 'appeasers' would find themselves shunned for quite some time.

Divergences of opinion among the strategy-making elite can lead to attribution error, especially when dealing with autocracies: for example, in May 1941, when Britain was at war with Germany, the attempt of Rudolf Hess to initiate peace negotiations by flying a small aircraft to Scotland was thought to have been authorized by Hitler, when it was not.

After the end of the Second World War in Europe, the hostility between the Greek communists and the Greek royalist government flared up into civil war. The British, who supported

The Rational/Irrational Actor Fallacy 25

the royalist regime, could no longer afford this burden and sought to discharge it upon the vigorous Americans who were still dithering between another withdrawal into isolationism and a commitment to playing a world cop in future. The British cry for help to contain the spread of the influence of Soviet communism in Greece and elsewhere was eventually answered with the Truman Doctrine of 1947, a commitment to stand by governments threatened from within or without by communist subversion.

At the time, western diplomats and defence analysts assumed that the 'satellite states' of the Soviet Union in Eastern Europe – Poland, Hungary, Czechoslovakia, Romania, Bulgaria, Yugoslavia, Albania – and the communist parties of other countries (including the Greek communists) were all acting in perfect obedience to Moscow's and the Communist Information Bureau's instructions. The assumption in the foreign ministries of Washington, London and Paris was that, worldwide, communism was a monolith. Then the Tito–Stalin quarrel of 1948 disabused them of this notion. They began to figure out that it was not Stalin but Tito who was supporting the Greek communists, while Stalin was trying to rein in both.[15] This led to the realization that there might be internal opposition from communists to communist regimes in Eastern Europe and, among them, to Moscow's orders. In due course, instructions went out from the Foreign Office to British diplomats no longer to use the term 'satellite' for the East European countries but where possible to explore and exploit differences.

Box 1.2: The Tito–Stalin Quarrel, 1948

In the early post-Second World War years, Stalin wanted communists worldwide to be singing from the same song sheet. It angered him when individual leaders of allied states started to do their own thing. One such leader was Josip Broz Tito

26 The Rational/Irrational Actor Fallacy

of Yugoslavia, whose approach to spreading communism was closer to that of Trotsky than to the more cautious approach of Lenin and Stalin. He was the proud leader of the communist resistance in Yugoslavia that had pinned down several German divisions during the Second World War, and he did not owe his position as president of the country to Stalin, unlike the leaders of other East European countries who had spent the war in Moscow.

Across the border from Yugoslavia, communists in Greece had also fought both the Germans and the royalist regime in Greece during the Second World War; this civil war had not burnt out, and in 1946 it flared up again. The Greek communists were crucially supported by Tito, who was keen to spread communism throughout the Balkans. In other ways, too, the Yugoslav communists were a thorn in Stalin's flesh as they had held out most valiantly against the Germans during the war. Proud of their martial achievements, after the war, they were reluctant to subordinate themselves in military matters to orders from Moscow. In June 1948, at Stalin's orders, Tito and the Yugoslav Communist Party were expelled from the communist community (the Cominform) in the hope that Tito would be toppled by communists loyal to Stalin. The attempted putsch failed, and Tito and his loyal supporters, although 'excommunicated' by the Cominform, refused to give in. Eventually accepting arms aid mainly from the United States,[16] Yugoslavia continued to be a communist state but independent of Soviet tutelage, later becoming a founding member of the Non-Aligned Movement.

Even autocracies can contain a variety of views within their own governments, usually more difficult to distinguish. Monolithic actor fallacy also led to misinterpretations of events in the context of another theatre of confrontation between America and the communist world, the Far East. In November 1950, in the first year of the Korean War, American

The Rational/Irrational Actor Fallacy 27

intelligence failed to realize that China was about to intervene on the side of the North Koreans. Already that summer, not long after North Korea had attacked South Korea on 25 June, hundreds of thousands of Chinese soldiers had been moved to the Chinese–North Korean border and, from October, small incursions were launched. The Central Intelligence Agency (CIA) in its Intelligence Memorandum 302 of 8 July 1950 assumed that it was Stalin who had originally ordered the war to take place, rather than the initiative coming from North Korea (the tail, it was assumed, could not wag the dog). The Memorandum also discussed the possibility that Stalin might employ Chinese forces to support North Korea, but thought this unlikely unless both Stalin and Mao were prepared to risk a third world war.[17] Instead, it was assumed Stalin was employing 'salami' tactics by bringing slices of the free world under his domination. Despite further evidence to the contrary reported in further intelligence memoranda, the US Intelligence Community also seems to have been put off the scent by Chinese foreign minister Chou-En-lai stating that 'volunteers' might come to support North Korea, probably so as not to be seen actually to be engaging in warfare as a state.[18] Stalin was indeed initially hesitant to grant permission to Mao to send regular armed forces into Vietnam, and there was also a heated debate among China's communist leaders as to whether to invade Vietnam; while eventually Mao's will prevailed over the Stalinists among his colleagues, this was not a foregone conclusion only a year after the communist regime had established itself.[19]

It is thus not only allied regimes – Yugoslavia, like all the other 'satellite states', had a bilateral treaty of mutual assistance with the USSR in 1948 – that might have their own agenda, at least up to a point, to the irritation of their partners. It can also apply to parts of the same government, as we shall see in more detail when discussing bureaucratic politics in chapter 4. In this context, one should point to the challenge to analysts of picking up on 'red-on-red deception', not only within an alliance but perhaps also within one state. Effects of the rivalry between different parts of the government (something that was typical of the Soviet Union, plus a factor in the all-pervasive Communist Party) can range from different sectors hiding from each other facts such as their actual expenditure to carrying out clandestine operations without informing other key decision makers. Even in open societies, decision makers are known to leave members of their government out of the loop deliberately from time to time.

An early assault on the assumption that states act as monoliths was very successfully made by Graham Allison with his study of the Cuban Missile Crisis.[20] He shone the light on several aspects of this 'Caribbean Crisis' (in Soviet terminology) that occurred in 1962, widely seen as the point in the Cold War that came closest to turning it into the Third World War. The decision making within John F. Kennedy's administration, examined by Allison, demonstrated nicely how different actors, in part representing different institutional interests (the State Department, the Department of Defense, the Chiefs of Staff, representatives of the Intelligence Community, the Attorney-General), argued for different strategies. Similarly, James Scott's study of American interventions in crises and proxy wars of the 1980s illustrates the many different positions taken by different members of the successive Reagan administrations on each of the several cases examined. The differences we find in the context of the Cuban Missile Crisis are thus typical rather than exceptional.[21]

To assume coherence in all government statements and actions is particularly misleading when important individuals are deliberately kept in the dark about developments by key strategic decision makers. During the Cuban Missile Crisis, in Washington, Soviet Ambassador Dobrynin was initially unaware of his government's deployments of nuclear weapons to Cuba.[22] In early 2022, when Russian President Putin used a

The Rational/Irrational Actor Fallacy 29

military exercise to prepare for the all-out invasion of Ukraine by regular forces, Belarussian partners and even high-ranking Russian military commanders seem to have been under the misapprehension until very late that this was indeed merely an exercise (albeit a rather exceptional one) which, it seems, accounts for the small fuel reserves and other shortcomings of the actual invasion. Leaving commanders and diplomats or even ministers uninformed about what is actually going on is easier for autocracies to do than for democracies, of course. It should not be assumed, however, that it can never be the case in the latter, particularly when coalition governments and political rivalries are involved.

Box 1.3: The Cuban Missile Crisis of 1962

In 1961, the United States under President John F. Kennedy deployed Jupiter missiles capable of reaching Soviet territory in the north-east of Turkey, America's NATO ally. This clearly spooked the Soviet government, then headed by Nikita Khrushchev. The USSR in turn had an ally in the Caribbean in the form of the new communist government of Cuba under Fidel Castro. As a counter-move, Khrushchev decided in 1962 to deploy missiles on Cuba capable of reaching well into US territory, which in turn greatly upset the US administration. Events became very tense when Kennedy decided to impose a 'quarantine' on Cuba, threatening to fire at ships transporting the Soviet missiles to Cuba – which would have been tantamount to the US going to war against the USSR. This measure was the result of deliberations by Kennedy and his chief advisers, who held a variety of views: which strategy to follow – confrontation risking an escalation to nuclear war, or compromise or complacency, which would have accepted, in the long run, Soviet missiles within range of America's East Coast cities – was dangerous guesswork on their part. Eventually, Kennedy made a secret deal with Khrushchev which resulted in Soviet ships turning back and, after a discreet delay so as not to make the connection too obvious, in the United States withdrawing its missiles from Turkey. This process was completed in 1963.

In the light of the American removal of its weapons from Turkey, one might think that Khrushchev's decision was smart, but the way the crisis over Cuba ended in the public eye made him look like the loser in this confrontation. A year after the crisis, he was persuaded to resign his office, too early to be able to claim the credit for the withdrawal of the Jupiter missiles from the Soviet Union's border with Turkey.

What was demonstrated by Allison was the heterogeneity of positions taken among Kennedy's collaborators, and the strong element of bargaining and compromise, not only in the negotiations between Washington and Moscow but also within the US administration. The process by which the decision was arrived at involved multiple actors with sharply differing opinions. Given the presidential character of the US Constitution, the US president made all the key decisions, excluding several members of his inner circle of advisers. This is more easily done in a presidential system, that is, a system that turns very largely on the powers of one person. In the United States, the president's powers are checked by the powers of Congress, but that was not much involved in the Cuban Missile Crisis. In other presidential systems, the president can find him- or herself confronted with an opposition majority in parliament after an election, and even with a government of the opposition party, in France called 'cohabitation'. By definition, coalition governments are not monolithic; coalition agreements made at the beginning of coalition governments rarely weather the test of unforeseen crises well. In short, the coherence of a government's actions depends in good part on the constitutional structure of that state.

As demonstrated by a burgeoning literature looking for 'bureaucratic politics' as a spoiler for coherent strategy making

The Rational/Irrational Actor Fallacy

in democracies and even in autocracies, focusing on bureaucratic reasoning comes closer to explaining it than one based on the monolithic actor fallacy.[23] Bureaucratic politics – different members of the decision-making elite, however smart they are, defending different interests that have little or nothing to do with the crisis or war in hand – can have huge repercussions. I shall discuss this in more detail in chapter 4 when examining the difficulties of producing coherent policy or strategy.

The delusion that governments are monolithic actors and its ensuing blindness to nuance is exacerbated by habits of expression. The NATO jargon that equates governments with the populations of their states by referring to 'nations' is particularly misleading in this context.[24] The continuing German trend in military circles to speak about 'the Russian' – in the Anglosphere at the beginning of the twentieth century, people spoke about 'Jerry' or 'Johnny Turk' or 'Ivan' in that way – is particularly inappropriate. This crude way of trying to capture differences in strategic culture is so lacking in nuance that it is unhelpful to analysis. And while it is of course appropriate to speak of an earthquake occurring in Afghanistan or Chile (as a geographic descriptor), we still often refer to 'Ecuador' and 'Thailand' when all or parts of the government are meant. It is a convenient shorthand, but it disguises and smooths over a complex reality, making it easier to think of countries and their governments as unitary and united in belief and purpose. Worse still, most (academic!) theories of International Relations treat states as unitary actors, failing to delve into the detail of who is who among their leaders, who might be opposed to such policies within the populations and whether there are influential opposition parties or movements.

32   The Rational/Irrational Actor Fallacy

Understanding structures:
The influence of institutions, parties and individuals

In democracies, decision-making bodies have an interest in giving more people the impression of being consulted than are actually involved, or carry real weight, in the final decision. As a result, many more people tend to claim that it was really they who drafted a (successful) strategy or initiated a (successful) policy than could possibly have done so. By contrast, if they are unsuccessful, all sides will claim that their initial advice in its pure form would have been the right solution but was not applied to the full, was watered down or dismissed, thus leading to failure. In this context, too, many claim to be the fathers of success, while failure is an orphan.

How does one establish who really has leverage and influence? The Kremlinologists of old did a good job finding out who mattered, following in detail as far as this was possible the promotions and demotions of those at the centre of power, and tracking their particular views. Analysis here might usefully address two levels: that of institutional leverage, and that of personality (the latter of which is less easy to fathom). The institutional distribution of power and attribution of competences[25] between government organs, political parties, other powerful interest groups (e.g., industry) and individuals differ hugely from country to country and must be understood in detail if one wishes to comprehend decision-making processes. The British political system, with its traditional one-party government and its often quite strong governments, can blind the superficial observer to the importance of political parties or parliaments in other governments. France and Germany, by contrast, only ever have coalition governments, which creates an in-built potential for divergences between ministers from different parties. In both countries, a small party vital to the survival of a coalition in government wields disproportionate power, and disputes on any political issue within that party,

The Rational/Irrational Actor Fallacy

projected into the government, can be of great consequence. At the time of the Kosovo crisis of 1988–9, the Green Party in Germany and the Greens and communists in France had a considerable potential for influencing and perhaps undermining their governments' stance on the use of force in the Balkans. Moreover, the structure of (usually two-party) government coalitions in the Federal Republic of Germany, which traditionally accords the chancellorship (head of government) and the defence ministry to the larger coalition party and the foreign ministry to the smaller, pre-programmes tensions and divergences between these. The differences in institutional culture between the (predominantly military-staffed) ministry of defence and the (diplomat-staffed) foreign office are thus systematically aggravated in Germany by the differences in party ideology between their respective ministers. This has been true for virtually all governments of the Federal Republic of Germany since the 1950s. Consequently, there is a tendency for the two ministries to keep each other in the dark over policies and initiatives, and a common government line was and is much more difficult to produce in Bonn or Berlin than in London. Location adds to this pattern: in London, officers and officials merely cross the road – Whitehall – to attend meetings in the other ministry; in Paris, Berlin and Washington, the ministries are a bus or a metro ride apart.

The particular structure of the American government is so well known for it to suffice here to draw attention to the characteristics that make this democracy's decision-making process and distribution of decision-making power so different from that of most other democracies: the great powers of Congress that allow it often to act as a separate policy-making body; the power of the president, checked only by Congress; and the openness of the policy debate. This last characteristic makes the United States a particularly difficult partner to work with, as the delicate compromises publicly arrived at in Washington leave barely any room for manoeuvre to take into account the needs and views of allies. Moreover, as the international historian Zara Steiner brilliantly demonstrated, the individual government agencies in the United States are so large and manifold that institutional competition within the government dominates policy making. Eventually, a compromise is arrived at within Washington, but it is brittle in the extreme, leaving its representatives in international organizations hardly any room for concessions.[26] Effectively, this gives American representatives a strange sort of power through ostensible weakness: they tend to look weak wielding it vis-à-vis allies: I once heard a British diplomat, in exasperation in one late-night NATO committee meeting, say, 'the British foreign secretary Lord Palmerston once quipped, "If I want to negotiate, I send a diplomat; if I want to send a message, I send a messenger". Which are you?' But weak as they may come across, American diplomats can thus force US positions on their allies if the latter don't want extensive stalemates. Alternatively, US representatives in NATO might simply thump the table and rant about free riders, but such a robust approach creates more resentment and is a less elegant way of bringing allies alongside. If again we keep such peculiarities in mind and are prepared to find more in other states, particularly states of a non-democratic sort, this will lead to suitable caution about the attribution of influence to different actors or sectors of the government, and it will give greater insights into who actually has institutional leverage and who does not.

This caution must be increased further by awareness of techniques which smart decision makers and their staffs have in keeping rivals 'out of the loop' or, more confusingly, in keeping them under the illusion that they have taken part in the key decision-making session when, in reality, the crucial meeting took place in a much smaller inner circle beforehand. Another conscious policy measure is to give them the feeling that they have been consulted and listened to, when they were seen only by junior staff and fobbed off with remarks about how right

The Rational/Irrational Actor Fallacy 35

they were and how much attention ministers had given to their views and were possibly given an advance glimpse of some draft paper, coupled with the usual injunction not to tell. They will walk away, filled with the satisfaction of believing themselves to be part of the holy inner circle that is 'in the know' – it is surprising just how many people fall for it.

The same can be said for states. Not having been invited to the tripartite Yalta meeting between Stalin, Churchill and Roosevelt, the French resistance forces' leader Charles de Gaulle not only felt snubbed but suspected that bad things had happened there behind his back. He later falsely accused Roosevelt of having 'partitioned the world', with Stalin at this meeting. Roosevelt's universalist values and worldview would never have permitted such a deal, giving away the right of other countries to self-determination.[27] Instead, what had happened was that in the previous October (1944), Winston Churchill with his nineteenth-century great-power mindset had visited Stalin in Moscow and on a sheet of paper had noted down the proportions (or 'percentages') of influence which the USSR and Britain should respectively have on the liberated countries of Europe: Romania, Bulgaria, Hungary, Yugoslavia and Greece.[28] Thus was created the myth of a 'Yalta Agreement' between America and the Soviet Union.

After the end of the Cold War and the collapse of the Warsaw Pact, in an effort *not* to decide their fates over their heads as Churchill and Stalin had done, and to reassure the East European countries that had escaped from Soviet domination, western diplomats tried to involve them in international organizations, especially in the European Union (EU) and the Organization for Security and Cooperation in Europe (OSCE). When they persisted in seeking NATO membership in the 1990s and early 2000s, NATO created the Partnership for Peace as an alternative to membership in an attempt to keep them at arm's length for as long as possible. This was supposed to give them the feeling of being involved in NATO through

36 The Rational/Irrational Actor Fallacy

endless committee meetings, at least some of which had little content. In the end, they did not fall for this subterfuge but continued to clamour for full NATO membership, which, reluctantly, the Alliance conceded in the years of 1998–2004.

It cannot be overemphasized how much weight is carried by collective institutional vested interests. The way in which NATO has re-invented itself in its collective struggle for survival in the post-Cold War world is only the tip of the iceberg – albeit a very remarkable one – in this context. Every part of any organization has a vested interest in proving its importance and in claiming that it makes a great contribution to the whole (usually coupled with the argument that it is under-resourced and understaffed in view of its importance). There is thus an equally built-in tendency for all embassies to argue that they are at the centre of the cyclone, or for all parts of a government, international organization or other parts of administrations to argue that it is their work on which the survival of the state, the world or, more importantly, governments depends.

Turning to personalities, these are usually the most difficult to assess. Under the system of the French Fifth Republic, the president alone was generally the supreme decision maker in all areas that truly counted, particularly in defence. Hardly anybody imagined just how much President Jacques Chirac of the centre-right RPR party would weaken his own position by the bad decision to call an election in 1997, which brought the Socialist opposition to power. Thereafter, French government decisions on defence were made mainly by Socialist Prime Minister Jospin and his government, with the president of the Republic hovering in the wings. This is just an extreme case of a shift of influence or responsibility between prime ministers and their defence and/or foreign ministers in many countries, depending on the personalities involved and on their personal interests. Much ink has been shed by historians about whether it was President Eisenhower or his Secretary of State, John Foster Dulles, or whether it was John

The Rational/Irrational Actor Fallacy   37

F. Kennedy or his Secretary of Defence Robert McNamara, who made key Cold War decisions, or whether it was Ernest Bevin or Clement Attlee in Britain, and what roles Anthony Eden or Harold Macmillan played as foreign secretaries, and so on. Personalities use structures differently, and the working of governmental structures differs from government to government, even within the same state. It is thus necessary to pay attention to the changes in process which new governments or ministerial reshuffles bring along with them and to the dynamics of relations between particular personalities.

Moreover, what is called the 'chemistry' between people is peculiar to each set of actors, be they in politics or the staff of a crèche. We all know from our personal lives how some individuals grate on us, and we no doubt on them. In politics, as in the military and in all parts of government, individuals are often forced to work together, despite the 'chemistry' between them 'not working'. By contrast, some combinations or groups of decision makers may get on exceptionally well, develop a supremely trusting relationship, correctly anticipate one another's moves and preferences and generally form a great team. The latter is said of General Ulysses Grant and US President Abraham Lincoln on the one side and of General Robert E. Lee and Confederate leader Jefferson Davis on the other side of the American Civil War. It is also said about British Prime Minister Winston Churchill and his chief military adviser, Field Marshal Alan Brooke, the later Lord Alanbrooke, even though their relationship was quite a stormy one. It was there in the cooperation between French President Charles de Gaulle and German Chancellor Konrad Adenauer in the 1960s, between their successors Giscard d'Estaing and Helmut Schmidt in the early 1980s, and then François Mitterrand and Helmut Kohl.

38　The Rational/Irrational Actor Fallacy

Legacy policies and external driving forces

What can be observed of a government's policies or strategy from the outside may include 'legacy policies' – policies initiated previously, usually by previous governments, which have never been terminated even though in the meantime there has been a comprehensive revision of overall policy or strategy. Thus in the early years of detente (1963–1979), when the United States and the USSR first began to talk about arms control, aiming to put a cap on or even reduce their respective nuclear arsenals, the nuclear weapons laboratories of both countries continued to churn out missiles under contracts that had been approved previously. And there may be 'silos' of decision making. Such stove-piping and policy making in silos can result in uncoordinated statements and actions, in turn creating perceptions of the dishonesty of such a government. 'False causality attribution' or 'fundamental attribution error' can fuel the (sometimes justifiable) suspicion that government spokespersons are consciously lying if parts of the government are doing one thing and yet the spokespersons claim the opposite. Sometimes the left hand really does not know what the right hand is doing and is deliberately kept fumbling for the light switch.

Other than the diverging or even clashing interests of those involved in policy making, there can be further pressures on a government that are not visible from without. One, particularly relevant to war and peace, can arise from cost calculations and (often skewed) perceptions of windows of opportunity that might close at some stage.[29] The former arises always when forces are mobilized beyond normal peacetime strengths. While the economy of Rome in Caesar's times could afford to keep soldiers in the field in winter quarters, European medieval wars tended to be seasonal (i.e., campaigns had to cease in winter, even if the war itself dragged on) because the much smaller medieval economies could not sustain armies for such

The Rational/Irrational Actor Fallacy

39

stretches of time. The soldiers would have to be sent home for Christmas.

Even in early modern times, as modern states with comprehensive tax revenues had not yet fully unfolded in Europe, raising an army for overseas action, and especially putting a fleet together for its transport, and then keeping both in port for several weeks was as expensive as actually going to war. There was thus a bias in favour of action once the means were assembled. Concomitantly, taking the decision to raise an army, if one did not have a standing army (this applied to England until Cromwell came along in the seventeenth century, and then again thereafter) was a huge economic gamble. Before England acquired permanent armed forces, any war involved raising soldiers and ships through private investment. For the investors, it was just about as damaging to pay for forces, if they were then *not* brought to action but consumed food and money, than to lose them in war. Acting, giving the investors a gambling chance of winning, was the preferred option in a naval warfare context where prizes taken were supposed to pay for the investment in a fleet, something that ended only with the Paris Declaration that in 1856 outlawed this. In state-on-state land warfare, making prisoners who could be held to ransom had ceased over a century earlier. But looting and plundering continued to be a popular pastime among poorly disciplined and badly treated soldiers.[30] It is still done by paramilitary or mercenary units or when regular soldiers' payments are in arrears.

Also, in recent times there could and can be pressure to use an expeditionary force once a certain point in its build-up has been reached in a crisis. The combined US–British air- and land Operation Market Garden, in September 1944, designed to roll German forces back from the Netherlands and push deep into German territory, was not called off despite late intelligence reports showing that the German *Wehrmacht* had far more forces in the area than originally estimated. The military commander, British General Montgomery, who had been urged to be more aggressive in his strategy by the Supreme Allied Commander, US General Eisenhower, estimated that it was too late to postpone the operation. The operation incurred particularly high losses compared with what it achieved.[31] At the time of writing, one can only speculate what role such considerations played in Putin's decision not to turn Russia's exercises of the winter of 2020–1 into a full-scale invasion of Ukraine, but to put this off until early 2022.

At all times, it has been costly to mobilize reserves. In the twentieth and twenty-first centuries when aggression was feared, there would be no potential gains in offsetting these high costs if you were in a purely defensive mode and no attack materialized. Because mobilization is so costly and disruptive, governments are reluctant to call up reserves, or deploy regular soldiers over long distances, unless the need is extreme. One example of this was the Israeli government's unwillingness to mobilize reservists in October 1973, when an Egyptian-cum-Syrian invasion was in the offing but intelligence reports were misinterpreted (see Box 2.4: The Yom Kippur War, p. 88). Another example is that of President Obama's decision to call off an operation against Syria's regime in August 2013 after he had previously publicly drawn a 'red line', that is, threatened punitive action if Syria's President Assad were to use chemical weapons. In retrospect, proclaiming such a 'red line' was a bad decision, although taken by a very smart leader. When Assad did use chemical weapons against the insurgents and civilians among his own population, Obama did not implement his threat. The situation seemed uncertain; the American intelligence services were scarred by their misinterpretation of supposed intelligence in the war against Iraq that it had started ten years earlier, to the point of being reluctant to make predictions; there was no clear end state in sight that might have been termed a success; and the cost of the mobilization was increasing by the day.

The Rational/Irrational Actor Fallacy 41

One must also consider that external players or developments may force the hand of leaders even of great powers or superpowers. In its Indochina War (1946–1955), the French government was committed to supporting the corrupt government of Bao Dai in Saigon when that really did not help the overall cause and prepared the ground for further communist-led opposition. In 1979, the Soviet leadership had committed itself to such an extent to the support of the communists in Afghanistan that it was 'events in Kabul itself' that dictated Soviet involvement. As the British diplomat and Soviet expert Sir Rodric Braithwaite summed up in his study of the Soviet intervention in Afghanistan, 'Step by step, with great reluctance, strongly suspecting it would be a mistake, the Soviet leadership slithered towards a military intervention because they could not think of a better alternative.'[32] Thus the superpower USSR was put on the spot by its allies in a minor Third World country, and made a bad strategic decision.

Driven by a different agenda

Strategy making means making choices. Governments and other decision makers are likely, in many situations, to have different issues to address simultaneously, multiple goals and multiple end states to pursue and, in war, different theatres of action to consider. They may have to pull their punches in one theatre better to concentrate their efforts on another. Their strategy in the former theatre may thus appear illogical, not best designed to deal with that situation, but becomes more understandable when it becomes clear that this was not the priority. Especially where conflicts take place far away from one's own territory, and involve an 'exterior operation', as the French so helpfully put it, key decision makers may well estimate that completely different things directly affecting their own country – unemployment, social unrest, environmental problems – must be prioritized. The effect may be an utterly incoherent, ineffective and thus wasteful strategy adopted for some foreign theatre of conflict, where deployments are too small, ill-equipped and ineffectual, are made too late, and serve only to illustrate symbolical engagement. The bureaucratic compromise resulting may thus be incoherent and thoroughly irrational, but follows the logic of getting all parties to strategy making signed up to it. For NATO, the EU and the UN Security Council, the preservation of unanimity, or at least the absence of a veto, often justifies watering down joint positions, sometimes to the point of ineffectiveness. The faith in solidarity as a value in itself quite often predominates over other considerations. Strategy making in a particular crisis or context is thus often driven by other considerations external to it. Lessons drawn from past experiences – whether applicable or not – may be a distorting lens through which this new crisis is seen, there may be the strong desire to avoid repeating mistakes made in other circumstances in the past, and then there may be agendas of a completely different nature that can play into decision making.

Let us go back to the Kosovo crisis of 1998–9 (see Box 1.1, The Kosovo Crisis, p. 15). The expectation in NATO and among officials of NATO member-states from early 1998 was that what was about to happen in Kosovo would be similar to what had happened in Bosnia-Herzegovina. NATO member-states' governments and NATO officials were weighed down by the guilt of their non-intervention in the Srebrenica massacre of 1995. They were determined not to allow a repetition of such a massacre, and as open fighting had begun and 'ethnic cleansing' was underway, they felt morally obliged to intervene.

At no stage did any part of NATO's International Staff produce an analysis of the problem at hand in Kosovo in terms of what was actually needed to resolve that problem (one answer might have been that NATO had little to offer there; another might have been, as in the cases of Slovenia and Croatia, to recognize Kosovo as an independent state – neither

The Rational/Irrational Actor Fallacy

43

was considered in 1998). No analytical paper ever raised the question of whether NATO, or any of its many functions, was actually an appropriate tool to bring a solution to the problem. Instead of looking logically for an appropriate tool (which might well have led to the realization that there was none available, and that this problem was actually intractable), the assumption was automatically made that (a) this problem had to have a solution; and that (b) the solution had to be NATO. Indeed, the media and op-ed pieces contributed to this: what use was NATO now that the Cold War was over, it was asked in many places, if it could not deal with a small problem in a small corner of Europe? The question put in this way is just as logical as to ask what use is a hammer if it cannot be used to swat a fly.

From then onwards, decision making flowed from western preferences, not from an analysis of the needs of the situation. Western preferences were:

- to keep NATO's credibility intact, whatever happened, and with it the survival of the Alliance as a safety net against developments on a much more important level than the fate of Kosovo;
- to demonstrate NATO's usefulness even in areas other than Article V contingencies[33] (an armed attack on a NATO member), and therefore, if pressed to intervene in the crisis, to do so quickly and with a limited commitment;
- not to have to undertake a full-scale invasion of Kosovo, and thus Yugoslav territory, with boots on the ground and the likelihood of casualties among NATO forces;
- to avoid having to supply such ground forces, possibly from the air, something that in the geographic context and with the number of planes and lengths of runways available seemed much more challenging than the Berlin airlift of 1948–9;
- not to become embroiled in a military commitment without end;

44 The Rational/Irrational Actor Fallacy

- ideally – a bureaucratic driving force which is an essential part of bureaucratic inertia – to follow some precedent, rather than to have to invent new procedures (which would invariably raise legal questions, engender long debates and possibly protests). The closest precedent was, naturally, the peace enforcement and then peacekeeping deployment of IFOR/SFOR in Bosnia-Herzegovina;
- *preferably* not to create for oneself legal difficulties with the UN Security Council, and particularly with the Russians, by ideally deploying peacekeeping troops *after* receiving a mandate to do so based on a comprehensive peace agreement signed by all parties to the conflict prior to NATO involvement.

There was a rival preference in some countries to use the Kosovo crisis to let NATO shake off the self-imposed fetters of subordination to the United Nations (UN), to its Charter and its Security Council, by creating the precedent of intervention to prevent a 'humanitarian disaster'.

Many different possible scenarios had to be contemplated, but NATO political directives and hence, military planning, constantly came back to the preferred scenario of a Dayton-type[34] peace settlement to precede an IFOR/SFOR-type deployment of ground forces. Claims that the situation in Kosovo was quite dissimilar from that in Bosnia-Herzegovina, even though Milošević and the Serbs were one party in both conflicts, were unwelcome, if anybody ever voiced them at all. As was the argument that, three years after Dayton, the 'international community's' success in changing the hearts and minds of the ethnic separatists was disproportionately small compared with the enormous resources pumped into Bosnia-Herzegovina. Thus decision making flowed logically – not from problem-oriented analysis, but from institutional preferences. All efforts were put into coercing Milošević to sign up to the Dayton Agreement that confirmed Bosnia-Herzegovina's

The Rational/Irrational Actor Fallacy

independence, but left it with a geographically complicated structure guaranteeing the coexistence of two semi-separate ethnic entities within the state. Air strikes (which had purportedly 'forced the Serbs to the conference table' at Dayton in 1995 to end the war in Bosnia-Herzegovina) were threatened because they were and are quite wrongly believed to be wildly effective in changing dictators' minds and destroying any popular support the dictators might have enjoyed, and they involve a low risk of NATO casualties.[35] Air strikes – 'surgical', swift, with an in-built exit strategy – were the tool the West was willing to offer, and the problem had to fit the tool: nobody produced a good idea of what NATO might do to force the Kosovar Albanian delegation to sign. When no legal mandate for action à la Dayton could be agreed, the argument gained popularity among the NATO member governments that Kosovo warranted an intervention on humanitarian grounds to prevent a catastrophe. How the tool of air strikes was supposed to resolve the problem of ethnic hatred in Kosovo, however, remained difficult to explain, even though impressive resources both in NATO and in member governments were devoted to the public presentation of these policies in search of domestic and international support. When addressing the public, efforts are of course made to justify and explain such decisions not in terms of institutional preferences but in terms of a problem-oriented rationale. Historians will probably seek in vain in the archives for the acknowledgement of institutional preferences behind NATO's air strikes in the spring of 1999. It is useful to keep this example of an institutional, preference-driven, decision-making process in mind and to read it across to decision-making processes elsewhere, so as not to seek a logic which does not exist and missing the underlying reasoning that is the greater driving force, the unnamed elephant in the room.

To finish with the Kosovo example, it can also be seen as a turning point in western relations with Russia.[36] The relations between Orthodox Russia and Orthodox Serbia, with its Cyrillic script and Eastern Slav culture, had after Tito's demise turned into a patron–client relationship between the Moscow and Belgrade governments, based both on actual cultural affinity and geopolitical interests on the part of the leaders of the Kremlin. The Russian representative on the UN Security Council thus vetoed NATO military action against the Serb rump state of Yugoslavia. Yet the air strikes proceeded, after long deliberations among NATO members, without UN approval and were thus arguably contrary to international law (the NATO members' legal advisers argued that intervention to prevent genocide could be seen as legitimate, however, even if not fully legal). For the Kremlin, the chief consideration in attempting unsuccessfully to block NATO action was that Russia's prestige as one of the Permanent Five members with the veto power in the UN Security Council (that marker of being a great power) was at stake. The Russian leadership felt humiliated as it had not been able to protect its client state. Vladimir Putin, who came to power shortly after the air campaign, has never ceased to remind the world that the NATO campaign was illegal. His agenda, ever since, has been dominated by the desire to revive and strengthen Russia's great-power status as one that can block western action. The fate of the Kosovar populations was never at the top of a Russian agenda.

A further deeply troubling example of agendas external to a particular crisis spoiling any rational evaluation of evidence is that of 2003, when the American and British governments had set their minds on an invasion of Iraq to topple Saddam Hussein's regime. One of several reasons often evoked is the then US President George Bush Jr's desire to finish the 'unfinished' business left by his father, George Bush Sr, who, when US president, had authorized the liberation of Kuwait from Iraqi forces just over a decade earlier but had stopped short of sending his forces to Baghdad to overthrow

The Rational/Irrational Actor Fallacy 47

Saddam.[37] When the credibility of intelligence on the supposed Iraqi production of biological weapons was called into question by a Central Intelligence Agency (CIA) analyst, his line manager commented, 'Let's keep in mind that this war's going to happen regardless of what Curveball said or didn't say, and that the Powers That Be probably aren't very interested in whether Curveball knows what he's talking about.'[38]

Box 1.4: Curveball and Gulf War of 2003

'Curveball' was the codename of an Iraqi informer who approached the German secret service with supposed intelligence on Iraqi production of biological weapons. The story made up by 'Curveball' would be central to the testimony given by US Secretary of Defense Colin Powell at the UN in February 2003 to explain US reasons for invading Iraq.[39] The self-appointed informer's scribblings on a sheet of paper, when pressed to produce some sketch of what an Iraqi biological weapons plant might look like, were transformed by accomplished designers into convincing pictures of production facilities mounted on a lorry, and thus supposedly eluding western inspectors by means of their mobility. At some stage, the German intelligence agents handling Curveball smelled a rat but did not dare come clean about it with their allies. The governments of the United States and the United Kingdom were keen to use the Curveball material to make the case for the US-cum-British invasion of Iraq that year ('The Second Gulf War'). This took place against strong domestic opposition in both countries, and with their close allies France and Germany opting out, given their concerns about the legality and legitimacy of such action. The invasion in turn took the lid off internal tensions that exploded into a civil war. Jointly, the external intervention and the civil war are estimated to have cost the lives of 210,000 Iraqis, most of them civilians.[40]

48 The Rational/Irrational Actor Fallacy

Given what has been said about multiple actors, multiple considerations, legacy policies, driving forces external to any issue, indeed the great diversity of issues that any government has to handle at any point and that pull attention and resources in so many different directions, there is much reason *not* to expect coherent policies or strategies to emerge. Consequently, as American security specialist Steve Yetiv has nicely demonstrated, in his *Absence of Grand Strategy*, the theories so dear to most lecturers in IR often do a poor job of explaining strategy making. He demonstrated this in his analysis of US strategy with regard to Iran and Iraq from 1972 to 2005. What emerges is much more random, disparate and inconsistent than most theories allow.[41]

Nuclear deterrence

Finally, in dealing with rational actors, the subject matter of nuclear deterrence deserves particular consideration. Relying on nuclear weapons to deter an adversary from launching a conventional or nuclear attack means taking a risk – the risk that the very weapons intended to *prevent* a large-scale conventional or nuclear war will actually *bring on* the latter. As Robert Jervis puts it aptly, a key 'element in the belief about whether the risks would seem controllable is a judgment about the inherent limits of manipulation and prediction in human affairs.' If it is assumed that decision makers 'can make fine, complex, and accurate calculations' in which '[f]riction, uncertainty, failures of implementation, and the fog of battle do not play a major role', in which decision makers 'see clearly their subordinates are able to carry out intricate instructions, and the other side gets the desired message', then nuclear weapons can be used by threat or even detonation to deter, coerce, compel and cajole. If, however, one has little trust in all these variables aligning in a favourable way, then nuclear weapons can only (at best) deter the use of other nuclear weapons.[42]

The Rational/Irrational Actor Fallacy 49

Once the USSR owned intercontinental ballistic missiles, ever more authors saw the risks involved in brandishing nuclear weapons. Several acknowledged that a US or French president's or a British prime minister's threat of using them was becoming ever less credible, given the Soviet leaders' ability in an act of retaliation to destroy US cities. The American strategist Hans Morgenthau commented that most issues over which wars might be fought in the nuclear age

> are either so important from the outset or acquire such importance through accidents, miscalculations, or the dynamics of the conflict itself that neither side could reconcile itself to defeat without having used a maximum of force to stave it off. Once force has been committed to such an issue on however small a scale, the risk of escalation is ever present, first quantitatively within conventional force itself and then qualitatively from conventional to nuclear force. Thus the awareness of the irrationality of nuclear war – which, as we have seen, impedes the resort to nuclear force – also stands in the way of the use of conventional force in so far as the latter might be preparatory to resort to the former.[43]

Thus Morgenthau thought nuclear weapons would prevent any war between the nuclear powers. But perhaps this only held true for western leaders, not for a Soviet regime with different values: with infinitely less concern about individual human lives, it might risk hecatombs of deaths even on its own side to bring on the end state of a world communist society. If so, rather than preventing all war, such reasoning would make the West helpless in countering conventional aggression by the Soviet Union and the Warsaw Pact.

Thomas Schelling and Roger Morgan, leading American experts on nuclear deterrence, argued therefore that, for nuclear deterrence to work, there has to be the assumption that the deterrer is irrational, as nuclear war would be too

50 The Rational/Irrational Actor Fallacy

devastating for anybody rational to want to bring it on. Thomas Schelling identified the need to leave something to chance in order to make deterrence credible.[44] 'There are no intrinsic interests', Roger Morgan wrote, that are 'of sufficient value' to make 'inherently credible' a state's commitment to defend another if necessary by using nuclear weapons, against another nuclear power, and thereby putting one's own country at risk of nuclear retaliation. And he added, 'If deterrence often rests on the ability of deterrers to limit, inhibit, or suspend their rationality or their inability to promise not to do irrational things in the heat of the moment, then it would seem unlikely that the way governments practice deterrence is . . . adequately captured by a rational decision maker model.'[45]

But again we are confronted with the question of whether a strategy that to us seems irrational – namely, one incurring a high risk of nuclear escalation – might seem reasonable to adversaries. Counting on our self-deterrence, they might assume they could cow us into submission with some limited nuclear use that would not destroy all life in Europe and would still lead to something that could be presented as a triumph on their part. Nuclear deterrence postures are thus not 'fail-safe', as an eponymous novel written in 1962 by Eugene Burdick and Harvey Wheeler argued, popularized further by films based on the novel. This is not the place to launch into a discussion of nuclear strategy, but it needs to be emphasized that this area of strategy making is most uncomfortably affected by conjectures about rational and irrational actors.

Points of view

Robert Jervis has written outstandingly insightful studies of what has gone wrong in the past in international relations, leading to misperceptions, if not worse to war. In these, he underscored repeatedly that what goes on is likely to look very different from the vantage of different governments,

The Rational/Irrational Actor Fallacy 51

different actors and observers.[46] Rufus Miles, an American bureaucrat, summed this up neatly in the late 1940s by saying 'where you stand' on an issue 'depends on where you sit' in the government.

A good example of Jervis's argument is the 'points of view' advertisement for the British newspaper the *Guardian* dating from 1986. Shown in cinemas and on television, this short advertisement presented an identical sequence of actions as filmed by different cameras from different perspectives. Depending on the position of the camera, we see a man running, so far without any particular reason suggesting itself, and his baldness and clothes give him the image of a skinhead. In a second frame, we see him running towards a conservatively clad man with a briefcase – we might think, a businessman – who, as though he is being assaulted, raises the briefcase as a protective shield. So is the runner about to assault the latter? Finally, as the camera with the largest focus shows, we see that the runner is attempting to save the man with the briefcase from a pile of unsecured bricks about to fall on him from the building site next to them both.[47] That events look different when seen from different perspectives is partly unavoidable, as the different sides have access to different information and knowledge about their own and adversarial intentions, but also have different perceptions of the world, of themselves and of their adversaries. And these latter views are influenced by biases which, as psychologists have amply demonstrated, make all of us less than rational actors at the best of times.

2

Our Biases

Let us turn now to biases arising on our own side that furnish evidence that neither the objects of our studies nor we ourselves are fully rational or even logical and coherent in our thinking, as the 'rational actor' assumption would stipulate. In identifying biases that can colour, distort and misguide our analysis, we should here reflect on our own irrationality. Our thinking and acting, too, is 'bounded' by our cognitive shortcomings, our biases. This is not to say that these biases affect only us – several of them seem to affect all of humanity. But there are also those that are more prominent in some cultures than in others.

Mirror imaging

A fundamental flaw in our thinking is to assume that, because we would or would not do something, another would or would not do it either. In June 1941, three days before Hitler unleashed Operation Barbarossa, the invasion of the Soviet Union, the British ambassador to Berlin spoke to his Soviet opposite number about the *Wehrmacht*'s build-up in the East.

Our Biases

53

He opined that the military preparations observed were merely 'one of Hitler's moves in the "war of nerves"'. He dismissed the idea that these might be preparations for an attack on the USSR: 'I find it difficult to believe. It would be crazy!' The Soviet ambassador concurred.[1] On a lighter note, in February 1945, Stalin, by then recovered from his initial shock about the German invasion and fully on top of strategy making again, invited Churchill and Roosevelt to Yalta in the Crimea to discuss joint plans for the post-war world. The daughter of Averell Harriman, the US ambassador to Moscow, who was also present at this conference, recounts the following suggestive anecdote. The three statesmen met in the Livadia Palace, a summer retreat of the tsars of old, stately but ill-equipped with mod cons. Stalin, in search of such facilities, found the only one nearby occupied, but was pointed by Harriman to another at the far end of the palace, advice the Soviet leader followed as the matter was pressing. In doing so, the Soviet secret service agents present lost sight of him and panicked, fearing that he might have been kidnapped by the Americans and the British – a Soviet head of state, in his own country, a five-hour drive from the nearest airport![2] Arguably, this says more about the sort of actions the KGB considered taking themselves than about British or American intentions at the time.

Box 2.1: Stalin's Failure to Expect Barbarossa, 22 June 1941

In the late summer of 1939, as war between Britain and France on the one hand and Germany on the other became increasingly likely, the former reluctantly tried to persuade Stalin to form a pact with them against Germany. Hitler's foreign minister, Joachim von Ribbentrop, beat them to it, however, and the unlikely alliance-of-convenience between the communist USSR and Nazi Germany was signed on 23 August 1939 in the form of a non-aggression pact, with a secret annex in which the two signatories agreed to invade and partition Poland, while the Soviet Union would also occupy the Baltic states.

Given the fundamental enmity of the two ideologies, however, one might have expected this 10-year pact to expire sooner, and there are some indications that both sides considered breaking their side of the commitment. Hitler had already ordered plans for the invasion to be drawn up in December 1940.[3] At any rate, Stalin was somehow mentally unprepared for Hitler's betrayal in 1941, despite receiving multiple warnings that Hitler was preparing an invasion of the Soviet Union. The German invasion, code-named Barbarossa, began on 22 June 1941.

In the weeks up to that date, Stalin dismissed more than a hundred reports from his agents (and even warnings issued by the British government) as to German preparations. One Soviet agent, Richard Sorge, in March 1941 informed Moscow of the German preparations, and on 15 June he telegraphed that the invasion would begin on 22 June.[4] Stalin not only dismissed this information, but was so firmly entrenched in his denial that he was caught completely unprepared, even mentally. He slipped into a depression, not appearing in public again until 3 July 1941. Meanwhile the *Wehrmacht* made fast progress with its *Blitzkrieg* invasion. This was arguably the worst analytical failure of all time.

More seriously again, in 1962, the CIA (that had been created only in 1948) failed to foresee the possibility that the Soviet leadership, feeling threatened by American nuclear missile deployments on its borders in Turkey, would resort to comparable deployments near the US border – on the island of Cuba. As a US intelligence analyst who later became a historian teaching at Yale put it simply, 'We missed the Soviet decision to put missiles into Cuba because we could not believe that Khrushchev could make such a mistake.'[5] And a mistake it was, purely because Khrushchev, by all accounts a very smart

Our Biases 55

leader, badly misjudged the reactions of US President Kennedy and his advisers. This bias is also called the fallacy of 'transferred judgement', that is, projecting one's own reasoning onto somebody else.

In 1981, British ex-intelligence officer Douglas Nicoll was charged with reviewing British intelligence assessments produced by the government's Joint Intelligence Committee (JIC) which had failed to spot preparations for military action on a number of previous occasions in a timely manner. These included the Soviet-cum-Warsaw Pact invasion of Czechoslovakia to crush the Prague Spring in 1968, the Yom Kippur War of 1973, the Chinese invasion of Vietnam in 1979, an averted clash between China and the USSR also in 1979, the Soviet invasion of Afghanistan in December 1979, Soviet–Iranian and Iran–Iraq tensions where a Soviet invasion was called off in 1980, and preparations for a Warsaw Pact crushing of the Solidarność movement in Poland in 1980 and again in 1981. Had Nicoll written his study a decade later, he would have added the failure to foresee the Iraqi attack on Kuwait in 1990 (see Box 2.2, p. 56). Several of these military operations were deemed unlikely by British analysts, using a logic that would have obtained in British decision making. But concerns about world opinion or the particular reactions of one of the two superpowers were in fact brushed aside by the respective one-party state governments in the cases of the invasion of Czechoslovakia, of Chinese intervention in Vietnam, and of the Soviet invasion of Afghanistan.[6] Thinking in the same vein, many western commentators could not bring themselves to believe that Putin would order the go-ahead for a full-blast Russian invasion of Ukraine on 24 February 2022.

Faith in communication

Mirror imaging – or at least the assumption that the adversary shares a similar understanding of the world and that one can

56 Our Biases

find a common language – is also at the heart of faith in communication and signalling of a verbal sort. While our everyday lives should teach us that the danger of miscommunication is huge, accidents with horrendous consequences in terms of the cost of human lives have occurred and keep occurring due to misunderstandings in inter-governmental communication. One particularly famous one is the misunderstanding that occurred between Iraqi President Saddam Hussein and American Ambassador April Glaspie, in an interview in Baghdad on 25 July 1990. After listening to Saddam complaining about Kuwait's riches and supposed threats made by (tiny) Kuwait against Iraq, Ambassador Glaspie, clearly mainly concerned about the high oil prices to which these tensions were contributing, said 'we have no opinion on the Arab–Arab conflicts like your border disagreement with Kuwait,' and added, 'All that we hope is that these issues are solved quickly.' In talking about resolving the problem with Kuwait quickly, she meant by mediation, perhaps by Egyptian President Hosni Mubarak,[7] unaware that the message that came across to Saddam Hussein was that America was giving him the green light to 'resolve' the Kuwait 'problem', and quickly at that, so that oil prices could be brought down in the region. One week later, Iraqi forces invaded Kuwait.

Box 2.2: Iraq's Invasion of Kuwait and the First Gulf War, 1990–1

On 2 August 1990, Iraqi forces invaded the small but oil-rich neighbouring state of Kuwait. The West was caught by surprise, not least as there seemed to be a good rapport between Iraq's leader Saddam Hussein and western diplomats, but also because the invasion was masked by Iraqi military exercises along the border with Kuwait. Even so, Saddam Hussein had chosen a bad time. Coming in an exceptional period of good cooperation between the Soviet Union, on its last legs under

President Mikhail Gorbachev, and the three western states that were Permanent Members of the UN Security Council, the Council decreed that this was a breach of international law and authorized joint action against Iraq. The United States assumed the lead in a war to liberate Kuwait, joined by forces from 41 other countries.

One Gulf War later, in 2003, it was again the misunderstanding of statements and the misinterpretation of actions that led to war. We have already referred to the Curveball story (see Box 1.4, p. 47). What persuaded leading American and other western analysts that there was something in this story was that it came after years of feet-dragging on compliance on the part of Saddam Hussein, and his continuing reluctance to give the International Atomic Energy Authority's inspectors access to some of his sites. To western minds, this suggested he had something to hide (when in fact he did not), reinforcing the sense of urgency in Washington and London that something had to be done to stop Saddam. Building on many years' studies of conflictual international relations, Robert Jervis commented that participants in these 'almost never have a good understanding of each other's perspectives, goals or specific actions. Signals that seem clear to the sender are missed or misinterpreted by the receiver; actions meant to convey one impression often leave quite a different one; attempts to deter often enrage, and attempts to show calm strength may appear as weakness.'[8]

Misplaced faith in communication was also at the heart of an increase in tension in what would be the last peak of the Cold War, the early 1980s. This is the story of Topaz and a batch of other spies – mainly East Germans – in West Germany's government in Bonn and also in NATO's headquarters in Brussels. They were mostly known to western intelligence. But passing top-secret documents to the East (mainly East Berlin) by means of these spies seemed like a good way to keep down

East–West misunderstandings. If the Warsaw Pact leadership (all top brass Soviet generals and admirals and marshals) found that, according to even such highly classified documents, NATO was planning no attack on the Warsaw Pact, nor anticipated that the Kremlin was harbouring such plans, surely that should reduce tensions. This was a false assumption on the part of western analysts, at least where the Soviet and Warsaw Pact military leadership was concerned. Recent research suggests that communications between East Berlin's and Moscow's intelligence services was quite poor. Perhaps the information from Brussels never reached Moscow, as an archival study by Frank Pringle, a student at the University of Glasgow, suggests.[9] As noted above, the Soviet hawks were caught in their bubble of worst-case thinking, mirror imaging and conspiracy theories. (Fortunately, Soviet civilian experts specializing in the United States eventually got Mikhail Gorbachev's ear and convinced him that Washington was planning no agression.)

We even know that East German military intelligence closely monitored western exercises – including tabletop exercises in well-guarded bunkers, such as the nuclear-release request procedures practised in the annual international NATO exercise Able Archer. In 1983, one such exercise may have alarmed Warsaw Pact military leaders as a possible preparation for war, to the point of readying nuclear-capable aircraft, despite East German military intelligence reporting nothing unusual about the exercise.[10] The flow of what must have been calming intelligence from Brussels to East Berlin – that there was nothing unusual happening on the Western Front – did not stop the 'hawks' among the Warsaw Pact generals and admirals (including East German ones!) from constantly making alarmist statements about the dangers of surprise attacks emanating from western exercises, both in public and in the top-secret meetings of the Warsaw Treaty Organization's defence ministers and national chiefs of staff.[11] This was mirror imaging at its purest, given that this practice of using exercises to prepare actual attacks was adopted not only by the USSR but also by its clients, such as Iraq's Saddam Hussein (see Box 2.2, p. 56).

Materialism bias

While Marxism–Leninism enjoys little popularity outside China and North Korea today, its legacy in the West in terms of a materialistic interpretation of the world is curiously powerful. For example, over decades of teaching, I have found that the default belief among students in Britain, France, Germany and elsewhere is that the Crusades were proto-colonialist, capitalist enterprises revolving exclusively around gaining fortunes. Modern students project their own world's (real or supposed) secularism and materialism into the past and assume that any other stated reasons for the Crusades (or other military ventures) are excuses, hogwash and lies. Even if they themselves have a more idealistic approach to life, they assume the worst about everybody else.

Since the 1980s at the latest, however, extensive research and publications originating with Jonathan Riley-Smith and his prolific disciples have proved that, with some exceptions, the reality was otherwise: the aim to save one's soul by risking one's life to save fellow Christians was paramount.[12] And yet it is extremely difficult to get students – or the general public – to accept that the Crusades were, at least initially, not ventures designed to bring material gain and economic benefit to the Crusaders or to impose western colonialism upon the Middle East (remember, these areas had been part of the Christian Roman Empire before the Arab invasions!). This is very difficult to put across to today's students or the general public.

Box 2.3: The Early Crusades and Crusaders' Motivations

The crusading movement had its origins in the call for help against the Seljuk Turks coming from the Byzantine Empire and the kingdom of Armenia, set upon by the Seljuk Turks from the second half of the eleventh century. After the three centuries of more tolerant rule by Arab Muslims that followed the initially very brutal conquests of the seventh and early eighth centuries, Seljuk Turks coming from Central Asia invaded the Middle East and replaced the Arabs as rulers. They conquered Persia, the Levant, defeated the Armenian kingdom and made inroads into what was left of the Byzantine Empire. The Turks forced Christians in the captured lands and cities to convert, or else they killed, tortured or sold them into slavery. Moreover, the Turks had barred Christians from the pilgrim routes to the Holy Places – Jerusalem, Bethlehem – that had remained open under Arab occupation.[13]

The paradoxical mix of a pre-Christian Germanic warrior cult and Christianity had produced a violent culture in which most nobles, from minor barons to dukes and kings, were guilty of cardinal sins, especially of killing others – an act that, even if condoned as part of a just war, was seen as necessitating some form of expiation. The ingenuity of the call to embark on the armed pilgrimages which we call Crusades, coming from Pope Urban II in 1095 and then from his successors, was that it not only encouraged European warriors to go and help their brethren in the East – as an act of fraternal love among Christians. It also addressed the felt need to expiate sins, appealing to ideas of honour and service to their feudal lord (projected onto Jesus), providing the unique possibility of saving one's sinful souls as the reward for this extremely dangerous venture.[14] In most Crusades, the Crusaders themselves invested enormous fortunes in the enterprise – even in our times, imagine the cost of travelling thousands of miles by land and sea together with numerous retainers, and having to feed and supply yourself, retainers and horses over two or more years! Meanwhile, fear of death in battle or from accidents or disease was ever at your side. Total fatality figures among the Crusaders defy calculation as, especially for the early Crusades, documentation on the deaths of commoners is scarce and very incomplete. But even many of the aristocrats who set out did not return, including a French king and a Holy Roman Emperor. Studies of wills show that those who went on Crusades were very concerned to make provision for their families and possessions in case they died, and Crusades were high-risk ventures involving huge, anticipated financial losses for the Crusaders.[15]

By contrast, Venice, Genoa and Pisa made great profits. The Venetians, especially, egged on the Crusaders of the Fourth Crusade to abandon their original aim of liberating the Holy Land in favour of the infinitely more lucrative conquest of Christian Constantinople and the occupation of what was left of the Byzantine Empire. That the search for lucre was central to this capitalist venture is undisputable; the Italian city-states benefiting from the Crusades through the need for transport it created and the opening of markets in the East have perhaps more rightly been called 'proto-colonialist'.[16]

This materialist perception is also fundamental to 'realism', the school of IR theory with its roots in nineteenth-century German nationalism and Social Darwinism, which imputes all the worst selfish motives to adversaries. In the 'realist' theory of IR, it assumes a slightly different form. It supposes that all state leaders have an ambition to increase and maximize their power (or feel threatened by such ambitions of others and seek to maximize their own protection against such threats), while ideals (other than security from the encroachment of other powers) for which they might call upon their populations to make sacrifices do not count, are eyewash or are mere propaganda. This perception of the enemy – especially the class-enemy capitalists and imperialists – was shared by Marx and continues to be shared by his followers. A telling misunderstanding apparently arose in the 1990s when diplomats of the People's Republic of China negotiated with British counterparts the conditions of Britain's withdrawal from Hong Kong, which was to revert to Chinese rule after a century and a half of British rule. In a later eyewitnessed seminar, the British diplomats commented on the strong Chinese assumption that Britain and British business would make it their priority to extract all their money invested in Hong Kong to guard against any losses, while British diplomacy aimed above all to keep as much investment in and contact with Hong Kong in the hope of thus assuring the enduring special (more democratic) status of Hong Kong politics and life in general.[17]

A narrow materialist strand also dominates much western thinking and, with that, there is an obstacle to understanding cultures and regimes that are more deeply inspired by ideologies. This is captured in a throwaway line by David Coates, a British diplomat who served at the British Embassy in Beijing. Commenting on negotiations with the Chinese, he said, 'We are British and we do not look at principles, we look at the detail' of diplomatic disputes.[18] It is thus symptomatic of western materialism that it translates into a disbelief in ideals as driving factors, although it is somehow conceded that foreigners have 'ideology', while Britons have 'common sense'. This attitude – often shared by Americans – generally results in discounting the importance of ideology in another side's motivations, and in underestimating the willingness to make huge personal sacrifices for the sake of a religion or the glory of a nation.

Many westerners today find the power of religious faith difficult to understand. As for some of us in our high-entertainment western societies, it is already asking too much to sit through the boredom of a church service every Sunday; it is difficult therefore for us to understand that in other societies, daily

Our Biases

mass, or praying five times a day, may be taken for granted. How much more difficult it is for us to understand the religiously motivated suicide bomber! Robert Jervis, in his study of why US intelligence did not pick up well in advance on the Islamist takeover in Iran soon after the beginning of the 1979 revolution, identified as one key reason 'that analysts, like everyone else at the time [in America], underestimated the potential if not existing role of religion in many societies. . . . [I]t . . . seemed inconceivable that anything as retrograde as religion, especially fundamentalist religion, could be crucial.'[19]

Nor had they anticipated how Islamic fundamentalists would manage to take the lead in uniting the many rivulets of opposition to the Shah's regime. Communists had similarly taken the lead previously in resistance and independence movements in Europe, Africa, Asia and Latin America. Islamists would do so again in the Arab Spring of 2011–12.[20]

In Russia, the growth and spread of a nationalist-cum-orthodox messianism and cultural pride could be observed over the decade of the 2010s. Yet many commentators in the winter of 2021–2 argued that Putin could not possibly want to invade Ukraine as it would destroy all that Russia had built up both economically and in terms of lifestyle in the past three decades, at least for its educated upper and middle classes in St Petersburg and Moscow. While it might seem to western observers that Putin's decision to invade Ukraine was blatantly not in Russia's best *material* interests, this does not mean that for Russians the glory and status of their country would not be worth sacrifices. Russia's honour and glory may appeal especially to those outside the main cities whose living standards have remained low and who have never benefited from Russia's opening to the West in the 1990s and 2000s. Nor should one underestimate the ability of members of an educated elite to be inspired by metaphysical values. And finally, in 2019, 69% of Russians bought Putin's argument that others (America, NATO) were actively preventing Russia from achieving its true greatness (against 29% who did not); and 84% of Russians thought that 'The foreign policy of my country should represent its own interests without restrictions.' Most Russians polled had no interest in foreign policy as a vehicle for enforcing human rights (35% for, 62% against).[21] This did not preclude international collaboration in their view, however: in a survey from late 2021, 75% of Russian respondents thought their government should cooperate with countries even if they did not share Russian values.[22] In 2019, Russians were equally as supportive as unsupportive of military interventions abroad (48% on both sides).[23] Respondents to a further survey in late 2021 were less enthusiastic about Russia's active involvement in solving international problems (68%) than they were in 2019 (83%).[24] Russian views are difficult to gauge, given that the older generations remember how to keep their mouths shut when they are asked their political opinions, which may be one of the reasons for the apparent fluctuations of this Levada Centre statistic about Russian attitudes to the United States.

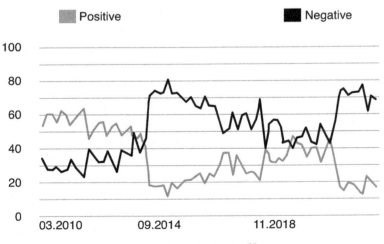

Source: Levada Centre[25]

Either way, Russian views on these questions are quite distinctive from those, say, of respondents in France or Germany.[26] So it makes little sense to project our views onto Russians.

Mirror imaging is also a bias affecting the Soviet and Russian leaderships in particular. The Soviet perception of the Euromissiles which NATO countries at the NATO summit in December 1979 decided to deploy in the following years was that, as *Soviet* strategists would use them as launch-on-warning weapons, so would NATO, notwithstanding what NATO spokespeople said about their doctrine in their top-secret documents (those might constitute *really deep* deception, might they not). The same interpretive approach was taken by Russians regarding the deployment of the NATO missile defence systems in Eastern Europe in the 2010s, which NATO members declared to be aimed at fending off a small number of potential incoming missiles from Iran, especially once it had become a nuclear power. Russian military commentators, looking at the system's technology, opined that the anti-missile missiles *could* be used with nuclear warheads in the role of Intermediate-Range Nuclear Forces (INF) and that, de facto, NATO was in breach of the INF abolition treaty of 1997. The Russian strategists applied worst-case thinking and assumed the West must be lying about its *real* intentions.

When western analysts failed to predict the Turkish invasion of Cyprus in 1975, or Saddam Hussein's invasion of Kuwait in 1990, or if there was disbelief even among some Russia experts that Putin would launch a full-scale invasion of Ukraine in 2022, it was not that none understood these regimes' reasons for acting. Nor can the regimes in question have been blind to the potentially bad consequences. But while many western observers thought these aggressive regimes would have been deterred from their acts of aggression by the negative consequences, the regimes in question had a different *prioritization:* they attacked *despite* all the negative reactions they might even have anticipated. And in the case of Cyprus, the Turkish

66 Our Biases

invasion succeeded in as much as Northern Cyprus is still in Turkish hands.

Confirmation bias

Confirmation bias is a bias we encounter in our daily lives as well as in foreign affairs and defence analysis. It plays to our need to make shortcuts in our thinking about how things work that alone enable us to function effectively, in a time-saving manner. One sub-category might be called the 'same as before' bias. My favourite example of this is an experiment described by Robert Jervis in which individuals are shown playing cards which they have to identify, in quick succession, such as the ten of spades, the seven of hearts or the ace of diamonds. After a short time, when the participants are well used to the routine, the experimenter introduces cards with abnormal colour combinations, a red king of spades, a black ten of hearts, and so on. It always takes the test participants a while to realize that something abnormal is going on, and, until then, they tend to continue calling out the name of the cards as though they showed their normal colours. We are trained to make such shortcuts to comprehension and under pressure may see only what we expect.[27]

We make assumptions about our environment and leap to conclusions about other people, and in the latter case we develop likes and reservations quickly and often stick by them. Questioned, we come up with evidence confirming this bias, blanking out evidence to the contrary. Worse still, there is the pattern, not unusual among historians and literary critics, which one might call 'falling in love with one's own theory'. I have found that when I had no particular opinion about subjects vaguely within my area of expertise but was asked to comment on them and espouse a position on the hoof (in a conference's Q and A, or an interview), I would be inclined to defend it. After all, my name was now associated with that response, I had a stake in it being 'right' and abandoning that view, let alone openly admitting to being wrong, would mean a loss of face, reputation and standing (even if nobody else cared at all). It takes not only integrity but also self-confidence to cleave to John Maynard Keynes's famous principle, 'If the facts change, I change my mind – what do you do?'

Confirmation bias is particularly toxic when it comes to analysing, not to mention anticipating, an adversary's intentions. Analysts will form a view as to what these are and tend to see confirmatory evidence, airbrushing contrary or ambiguous evidence out of their picture. They generally find it difficult to abandon their earlier interpretation for a new paradigm. 'Anchoring' is a subset of this phenomenon, when a first impression formed or first information given about a case conditions the way it is subsequently interpreted, causing reluctance to change one's mind in the light of divergent evidence.

Here a word might be said about translation and the interpretation of foreign languages. As anybody who has learned a foreign language knows, words from one language do not necessarily translate into another precisely but tend to bring with them a variety of connotations. Translations obscure this variety of different connotations and meanings as they settle for just one word. It is only from reading the original word or expression over and over in the original language (which, obviously, one must be able to read!) that one may gauge that it has a significantly different nuance in some contexts. The effect is, as Russia experts Dimitri Minic and Dima Adamsky have recently found, that reading a Russian military journal exclusively in English translation leads to misunderstandings. He highlights the employment of the term *стратегическое сдерживание*, usually translated into English as 'strategic deterrence', which in Russian can carry an aggressive, preventive connotation, to the point where it more closely resembles

68 Our Biases

what we might call 'coercion'.[28] This is quite an important difference. Confirmation bias – or should one say, recognition bias, the self-delusional assumption that one recognizes and understands the word – obscures these differences. One encounters the expression assumed to mean deterrence in the English sense, and fails to think again.

Nor is it enough, as I have found, to spot an expression in, say, English or French or Russian military literature that echoes a concept introduced by some earlier Prussian or Swiss thinker. Often, in translation, the concept acquires a subtly different meaning, as can be seen in the evolution of the terms *Ökonomie der Kräfte* or *économie des forces* which in Napoleon's time related to bringing the right forces to the right place at the right time and supplying them appropriately. It has since, in English usage, acquired a connotation of parsimony (and to the critical mind evokes the danger of over-extension). Over time and translated into different languages, a concept will adapt to its new context. For text interpretation, nothing, not even DeepL Translator, can be a full substitute for an intimate knowledge of the original language as it was used at the time of writing. We can never get entirely into another person's mind, but a good knowledge of their language and culture gets us a lot closer. This fact is incompatible with a swift rotation of diplomats or, much swifter still, of military personnel in and out of different countries and cultures, when they are nevertheless charged with intelligence or other country-specific analytical work.

Processing incoming information according to pre-existing interpretive patterns, fitting it into stencils, one might say, is the twin of resorting to prefabricated, off-the-shelf responses to events. A time- and reflection-saving procedural shortcut is to assume that a task one is given is the same or operates on the same principles as a previous one. Thus the military has its SOPs (standard operating procedures), so that procedures do not have to be invented afresh every time, and so that they

Our Biases

can be learned in advance of possible application and then applied by all without extra training. (Incidentally, our own or the adversary's SOP is a giveaway for analysts: the SOPs for the configuration of nuclear missiles applied by the Soviet military personnel when putting their missiles on Cuba alerted US analysts to their presence when scrutinizing photos taken by an American U2 spy plane. Mischievously, the American strategist Edward Luttwak pointed out that following SOPs makes one predictable for an adversary, and that therefore one's own disorder and mismanagement could be a good thing as it might just confuse an adversary about one's intentions.[29])

To speed up ingestion by decision makers, briefing papers of all sorts contain executive summaries upfront – a practice that caters for busy decision makers who must be able to glean the most important message in minimal time. Unfortunately, what gets lost in this habit is that what may end up being written at the beginning – 'Bottom-Line Up Front' – should in fact come *last*, not first, after the argument is presented for scrutiny. Confirmation bias is an illness plaguing the social sciences. Thus political science students are often made to produce abstracts and structures in their dissertation proposals or PhD applications, where these can only emerge from their subsequent research. My favourite *bêtise* in this regard is that of grant-awarding authorities and institutions asking applicants what findings they expect, to which the response, surely, must be that if one had a ready-made answer to this question, the research would no longer be needed or else would be blighted by a binary bias of either confirming or falsifying the answer. It would blind the researcher to seeing entirely different themes emerge from the research, requiring quite a different conceptualization of the issues in hand. This social science approach feeds a confirmation bias, with students and analysts now setting out 'to show that', 'to argue that', 'to demonstrate that', much as American and British intelligence agencies were persuaded by the Blair government in 2002–3 'to show that'

Saddam Hussein had weapons of mass destruction. This is not only at odds with the very purpose of academic inquiry but, in this case, even unethical behaviour; as such it has since been dissected and condemned in great detail by the Chilcot Commission in their Iraq Inquiry facilitated the British government's decision to go to war against Iraq in 2003.[30] And yet this approach still predominates in IR departments.

The 'same as before' fallacy usually means less effort is made to ascertain what is new and *not* as before. This can have terrible consequences, as another example involving Saddam Hussein shows. In her interview with him on 25 July 1990, US Ambassador Glaspie expressly said that the message she was asked to convey by her Secretary of State James Baker – to improve relations with Iraq but keep out of regional politics – was one she had already been given back in the 1960s in a previous posting in Baghdad.[31] Perhaps this assumption that she had the same mission as before in similar circumstances prevented Glaspie from listening closely to Saddam Hussein, and from picking up signals contained in the terms 'invasion' and 'threat' and 'defence' which should have rung alarm bells that this was a security-related situation that had a potential of blowing up in her face, not just a repeat of the 1960s.

Douglas Nicoll in his report on the poor performance of the British Joint Intelligence Committee in predicting military invasions also identified confirmation bias – sometimes known as 'perseveration' – as a reason. For example, the JIC clung to its estimate that the Soviet Union would not order the invasion of Czechoslovakia in 1968, even as evidence was amassing that this was being prepared.[32] Admittedly, it is not such a bias that is to blame when our own estimation of the would-be aggressor's strengths and force readiness and the would-be victim's strength differs from that of the aggressor's, because the would-be aggressor miscalculates these. As Nicoll put it in 1981, 'though our own assessments of military capability may be broadly accurate, it does not follow either that the potential

Our Biases

71

aggressor will make the same assessment, or if he does, that he will draw the same conclusion from it.'[33]

Anchoring countered by befuddlement

'Anchoring' leads to a particular form of confirmation bias. The term describes an early interpretation given to an event or a new actor on the stage, leading to subsequent interpretations being accepted or dismissed depending on whether they fit or disagree with this early interpretation. One can also count here a conviction about somebody or something that is proved wrong by several incoming pieces of information, to which one nonetheless clings. A recent example is that of Israeli intelligence being anchored in their belief that Hamas, the terrorist party that was brought to power on the Palestinian-inhabited Gaza Strip by elections in 2007, was finally turning into a 'normal' political party and was adapting to its duties as government. This belief was derived from Hamas's non-intervention in August 2022 and May 2023, when Israeli Defence Forces (IDF) attacked leaders of the rival Palestinian Islamic Jihad within Gaza. Moreover, it was assumed that IDF actions against Hamas in May 2021 had left Hamas not only licking its wounds but also deterred from any further attack on Israel. The opposite was the case: almost immediately, Hamas seems to have started planning its major attack on Israel for 7 October 2023. In the autumn of 2023, there were indicators gleaned from sensors in Gaza and observations of activity along the frontier of Gaza with Israel, relating to unusual activities, especially Hamas fighters training to attack models of Israeli tanks, military bases and of a kibbutz. As a result of the anchoring on the belief that Hamas was not up to anything, these were apparently dismissed.[34]

Russian television audiences are systematically confused, one might say, by a particular informational practice of discussing news so as to steer them away from the most obvious reading of events. The treatment of the plane crash that on 23 August 2023 killed Yevgeny Prigozhin, the leader of Russia's famous Wagner mercenaries, is a great example of this, as Masha Borzunova nicely demonstrates.[35] Prigozhin had shortly before attempted a military coup. With some of his mercenaries, he had moved on Moscow, challenging Putin's leadership even *if*, as has been suggested, he only wanted to be made minister of 'defence'. Russian TV spectators were put off the scent of a fairly obvious interpretation of the plane crash – namely, that it was shot down on Putin's direct or indirect orders as an act of revenge or punishment – by speculations made by multiple commentators. First of all, this most obvious interpretation that was made by newspapers throughout the West was discredited by Russian TV commentators as being 'scripted' by some supposed central news authority dictating to western media what to put out (*conspiracy! Secret powers behind the scenes!*). This very much overestimates the powers of western governments to control the media. Then Russian commentators ran through a series of alternative explanations – Prigozhin and his fellow passengers on the plane were military guys, and don't military guys carry explosives? Might a grenade in their baggage have gone off accidentally? Or this was a foreign plane and it was not serviced properly as it required foreign parts which were not available; *cui bono?* – who benefits mainly? Russia? No, as Prigozhin's fighters were so vital to Russia, so it must have been the Americans and the British who gave this 'present' of Prigozhin's death to Ukraine on the eve of Ukrainian Independence Day to give the demoralized Ukrainians something to celebrate, and so on. A rhetorical trick deployed is to say, 'I am not making any connection between A and B, but the coincidence is striking' – typical conspiracy theory stuff – and thereby planting (i.e., anchoring) that very association in the minds of listeners.[36] With all these alternative explanations thrown at them, spectators will end up befuddled, with only one narrative to help them make sense of these

Our Biases   73

many interpretations of the event: the big context, explained by the master narrative that the United States/NATO/Britain is at war with Russia by indirect means, aiming to weaken and humiliate Russia in every which way they can.

While the practice of exploring as many other interpretations as possible is a salutary exercise for intelligence communities, there is a danger of befuddlement there, too. Analysts may be on the receiving end of deliberately spread false information to put them off the scent of what is really happening, in the way that chaff is deliberately ejected around an incoming plane or missile to confuse radars as to its whereabouts. (Worth bearing in mind, too.)

Apes' ball games and dogs that don't bark

Analysts tend to develop sets of indicators to look out for to give them objective criteria for interpreting developments, and this is generally very useful. The late Michael Herman, a British pioneer in bringing the intelligence and academic worlds together by opening the former's methods of working to academic scrutiny, explained this to me just after the end of the Cold War. One might imagine a large board with lots of little sets of lights, green/yellow/red, representing observable actions and developments like the increased stocking of fuel, the movement of tanks to a particular area, the calling up of reserves, and so on, and analysts will watch these indicators, switching from green (normal) to yellow (increased) to red (highly worrying increase) as appropriate. The overall pattern of lights on the control board will indicate to somebody monitoring the board as a whole if a situation is becoming worrying or even very dangerous.[37] In the early 1980s, the Soviet Union famously applied this observation-by-indicators in their intelligence operation RYAN, in which agents were told to find out whether NATO countries were preparing a surprise nuclear attack on the Warsaw Pact. One indicator was the observation of lights on in the British Ministry of Defence's main building on Whitehall – were people working unusually late hours? Another was potential increases in blood reserves held by hospitals. In total, 194 indicators were listed.[38] As a friend who worked at the British Ministry of Defence at the time told me, this in turn spooked British analysts puzzling over what the Soviets were up to. (The indicators did not show up a pattern of war preparations at the time.)

Another very good example of publicly available indicators which would give an expert on the lookout the red alert that something is about to happen concerned Russian exports to the contested eastern parts of Ukraine, just prior to the commencement of the Russian clandestine war in these areas in the early months of 2014. Technical descriptions of old variants of the Kalashnikov (AKM, AK-74, etc.) show that the receiver is 'a U-shaped 1 mm thick sheet steel pressing supported extensively by pins and rivets'. Dr Rebecca Harding and Dr Jack Harding – two analysts in the private sector – studied Russia's exports to Ukraine in sectors that fit this description, using openly available export statistics. They saw an increase of 58.3% in 2013, before the annexation of Crimea, followed by a >300% increase after the annexation of Crimea but prior to escalation in fighting in the Donbas region. Russian exports of 'commodities not elsewhere specified' to Ukraine – as recorded less clearly in export documents – were an astonishing 15,000% higher from January 2013 to May 2014 than in the three years preceding the onset of the Ukraine crisis (January 2010 to December 2012).[39]

However, the eager search for evidence to back existing theories can at the same time make the analyst blind to other evidence potentially much more important than what they were looking for. A humorous study of this was made in the 'Monkey Business' experiment, a version of which has been put on YouTube by David Simons. In this experiment, students were asked to count the number of passes made in a ball game

Our Biases

by one team dressed in white. The other team was dressed in black, so there was a bias for those involved in the test to ignore it. At the end of the test, most students/spectators seem to have missed entirely that halfway through, a (black) gorilla walks into the picture, beats its chest and disappears again.[40] Watching out for one thing so intently can make you fail to spot something else that is actually more important – perhaps even the elephant in the room.

This also applies to in-depth studies. My Master's thesis at the London School of Economics concerned British, French and German policies to keep Turkey out of the Second World War, and in my usual thorough way I read every diplomatic document available on the narrow time period of 1938–9. Proudly talking about my dissertation later, I was asked whether I had come across any reference to Elyesa Bazna, an Albanian in the service of the British ambassador in Ankara who, under the codename of Cicero, passed information to the German embassy. This espionage scandal was of course the much more famous story in retrospect, which with my narrow time- and subject-focus I had missed altogether. Had I read just a little more widely to start with, I would have realized that the much more intriguing question was whether the German foreign ministry knew what their French and British counterparts were up to through the supply of such information by Cicero, and yet took no countermeasures because all sides had an interest in a neutral Turkey.

Related is the problem of noticing the significant non-occurrence, which is harder to detect than an event one can look out for. In a short story by Sir Arthur Conan Doyle, his master detective hits on 'whodunnit' when he realizes that in the theft of a horse, somebody working at the stables must have gained access to it, as the guard dog did not bark as it would have done with an unknown intruder.[41] But how to realize what significant thing did *not* happen?

Conspiracy theories

Russians generally love conspiracy theories. This also applies to other cultures with roots in one-party or theocratic societies where a belief system or a religion, taught by an apparatus of priests or polit-commissars or mullahs, purports to explain the world in Manichaean binaries of the Good and the Wicked. Conspiracies and conspiracy theories have a long history, and this is not to claim that cabals have never existed or putsches or *coups d'état* have never occurred, or that governments have never been overthrown by a small number of influential conspirators. Indeed, Russia, where elites resisted democratization for longer than other European powers, has a particularly rich history of such actual conspiracies, starting with the Dekabrists of 1825. More often than not, however, such conspiracies were imaginary, such as the one that led Tsar Ivan the Terrible to slay his own son.

The conspiracy lens has chronically and pathologically become a filter to many Russians' views of the world. It greatly underestimates individual agency and the drive that might move groups of dissatisfied people to rise up against their governments, which was the essence of the 'Colour Revolutions' in Eastern Europe after 1991 and of the Arab Spring, all of which have been attributed by Russian military authors and government documents to American machinations.[42] Yet demonstrations by frustrated citizens did and do also occur in western democracies during and since the Cold War, or in Israel throughout the spring and summer of 2023. While, during the Cold War, money flowed from the USSR through communist East Germany to anti-nuclear demonstrations in the West,[43] or while the Russian regime seems to have interfered in the British Brexit referendum in 2016 and the election of Donald Trump as US president in 2017, such interference does not *cause* these trends or movements. They usually only increase them marginally.

Our Biases 77

This faith in conspiracy theories has made the Russian leadership – including especially leading generals and other military thinkers – blind especially to what western democracies are like as political decision-making entities: very slow at deciding, contradictory in view of our bureaucratic politics, and so on. As a result, as Dimitri Minic has shown, Putin, his spokespeople and Russian military leaders all consistently depict an American-cum-NATO conspiracy which is out to harm post-communist Russia, even to break up the Russian Confederation as it now exists. In the early 1980s, Soviet military leaders – the 'hawks' – had persuaded themselves and sought to persuade others that all evidence emanating from the West as to NATO's peaceful intentions – including a very substantial reduction in numbers and yield of NATO's nuclear weapons and their replacement by a smaller number of cruise and Pershing II missiles with smaller yields and smaller circular error probables – were masking aggressive plans.[44] After the demise of communism in Russia, this has continued to be the hallmark of the Russian 'hawks'' interpretations of supposed American-cum-NATO masterplans – western 'hybrid war strategy' – to reduce Russia's influence in the world. This filter in the Russian hawks' view of the West and of the world is so deeply rooted that nothing the West can do can penetrate it to change their view. Back in the 1980s, there were, fortunately, also 'doves', mainly civilian foreign policy experts, who, with the change of regime from Brezhnev and Andropov to Gorbachev, managed to influence the latter to give peace and detente a chance. Forty years on, we see no sign of such doves in Moscow.

The greatest problem with such conspiracy theories is that nothing can break the hermeneutic blinkers of this confirmation bias. All evidence that could shed doubt on the conspiracy interpretation can be dismissed as deliberate deception, enemy attempts to blur the picture and to mask real intentions.

Theories, patterns and statistics

A historian by background who in her studies somehow escaped any exposure to formal IR theory teaching, I carry a burden of guilt towards a couple of my earliest PhD students who were deeply interested in IR theory: I took them to task when they presented me with chapters on how the events or ideas they intended to study were explained *either* by theory A *or* theory B *or* theory C. I opined that no theorist could be so daft as to think that only one of these theories revealed the entire truth, that 'there is no salvation outside this Church'. Surely IR scholars were aware, I said, that their theories taken together jointly explain the interplay of multiple causes leading to big events and developments. For that is how historians would go about such explanations. They would shine the light on the multiple factors, dynamics, drivers and restraints that would lead, say, to the outbreak of the First World War in July 1914, rather than during one of the several crises preceding it that could have tipped into war; or they would look for the complex reasons why the Spanish Civil War (July 1936–April 1939) that involved all the major combatants of the Second World War nevertheless did not actually trigger this war, and so on.

But in fact this is not how IR theorists approach a subject. IR theorists do indeed focus just on one theory, one causality, one explanation. That is also the focus of student essays, dissertations and theses, to the horror of historians: students are made to start with a theory, to undertake superficial case studies (often based merely on secondary literature in English) of real events to see if they fit the theory, and then either the theory is shown to be true, or 'falsified' and discarded, following the logic of Karl Popper's heuristics, that is, his theory of knowledge. As a third option, the little cogwheels of the theory are adjusted to ensure the theory (then usually called 'neo-somethingorother-ism') fits the new case. (This of course, as the 'Apes' ball games' section illustrates, is likely to blinker them to very different explanations that approach the question from an angle more appropriate to that particular subject.) Worse still, when a new (or adjusted, neo-) theory emerges from three case studies (say, of counter-insurgencies), it contains the bold claim that this theory will now apply to all other cases (say, of counter-insurgency operations).

IR theorists are usually aware that the procedure of testing a theory in the Popperian quest for a case that falsifies it is just a formal approach, a sort of game with no claim to provide a recipe for action by practitioners. Scholars who recognize that this is just a theoretical exercise modestly claim no applicability of their research to the practice of policy making. Some even go all the way and deny any positivist results from IR research, as everything we deal with is constructed in human minds anyway. But that then begs the question why it would be worth pursuing such studies. At any rate, practitioners do not see it that way when they are required – as is now increasingly the case – to come up with research results to support a particular course of action – e.g., a counter-insurgency strategy – they propose. Therefore, think of the danger inherent in a practitioner picking up a student thesis with its theory on counter-insurgency and its three case studies, and then drawing up a strategy on the basis of that thesis for a new case in hand in which all the parameters are different. (For counter-insurgency, substitute nuclear deterrence, prevention of terrorism, development aid, or the distribution of emergency aid to civilians in war zones.)

Let me suggest a different analytical approach, namely to identify *patterns*, and then to ask whether this can be applied to a new case in hand. To exist and to be of importance, a pattern does not have to be found in every case, nor does it have to apply always. For example, when a knee gives trouble, the main joint may be replaced without tampering with the kneecap because *for 85% of patients* this suffices. Unfortunately, the other 15% need the additional surgery on the kneecap. The fact that this applies *only* to 15% does not rule out that you are among them, and that your surgeon should perhaps look out for other evidence as to whether you might fall into this category instead of opting, purely on the basis of statistics ('baselines'), for the conservative operation. A *pattern* such as the one described may thus apply only some of the time, and yet be important for the case in hand. Moreover, this allows for contingency. The pattern in one thing may apply if other factors are present, requiring a more complex diagnosis – you may also show signs of a high this or a low that which then is often – not always, but often – correlated with being among those 15% who should have their kneecap tackled surgically at the same time as the rest of the joint. (And, yes, I am speaking from experience.)

A statistical approach wrongly applied may do as much damage to analysing an individual case as to resolving it. Focusing on the majority of cases is proper and probably unavoidable when health services or hospital planners allocate resources: they need to know how many places will *on average* be needed for intensive care, how many operating theatres, how many beds in maternity wards, and so on. They may be forced to reduce average days and nights of hospitalization after surgery in the light of overall savings imposed by a government. But individual physicians are well advised to reserve their right to judge whether some patients must be kept in a little longer.

While it seems cost effective to go for likely diagnoses and not order additional tests to rule out alternative illnesses, this can cost the lives of misdiagnosed patients. Think of this example. Most women afflicted by cervical cancer develop it well after the age of thirty. Statistically, it is therefore unlikely that women under thirty have cervical cancer, so why pay for the test? Consequently, from time to time, young women seeking medical help for abdominal irregularities or pain are refused

Our Biases

81

the relevant test because of the statistical unlikelihood of cervical cancer being the cause of their troubles (and in order to save the cost incurred by the tests); thus their cervical cancer, fatally, goes undetected and untreated.[45] This is the 'base rate fallacy', when we are concerned about individual cases and not the design of hospitals or health services' budgets. For a state, in the great scheme of things, such fatalities may be deemed acceptable; for the individuals concerned, they are tragic.

Project that onto decisions about war and peace, where flaws and mistakes can quickly mean the deaths of thousands, tens of thousands, hundreds of thousands. Calculations of statistical probabilities here are quite inappropriate for analysing an individual crisis or war. Rolf Dobelli is dead right when he notes that 'There is no such thing as an average war.'[46] Or, as Robert Jervis emphasized, 'When we talk about wars, both those that occur and those that have been avoided, we care about specific cases.' And while one might concentrate on the most likely ways in which a war could break out, any major war in the nuclear age would be so exceptional that it would almost by definition not fit any rule of likelihood.[47] Also, picture an analyst even of a more likely form of war saying, 'Sorry, this outcome of the crisis/war was statistically unforeseen – it differed from the three case studies on which we based our policy recommendation!' As one practitioner put it to me, 'A belief that elaborate compilation of comparative data series is or should be an important resource for real-world governmental security decisions would indeed be a rationalist delusion.'[48]

Instead of looking at theories or *statistics*, there thus seem to be advantages in looking for *patterns*. That *some* patterns recur is what the comparison of several, ideally many, cases suggest. Coming to a new case, the n+1st case, all that such comparisons can suggest is to formulate this question: do we find a previous pattern in the case in hand? Perhaps, but not as a rule: one must *not* assume that known patterns always apply. If one discerns that a pattern does apply in a case we are

82   Our Biases

analysing, a second step may be taken, namely to ask: what (if anything) worked in similar configurations in the past? Might it work here? But nothing replaces the detailed study of the present case that has to be made.

Having advised readers to look out for patterns, I need to add a caveat. We may be seeing patterns in clouds where in reality there is only suspended water. Most medical students tend to go through a phase of hypochondria: when symptoms of illnesses are described, sooner or later they think they discover them in themselves. Similarly, when a relatively exceptional event occurs, interpreting another as potentially similar is more tempting than if that earlier one had not recently been experienced by us. 'Availability heuristics' is a term used by psychologists to describe this phenomenon.

We have already mentioned the fallacy of assuming that every autocrat, every dictator, had exactly the same expansionist plans as Hitler. A police inspector specializing in murder and abduction cases commented recently that he is very wary of colleagues suggesting that they have seen it all before in other cases (other than when a serial criminal is at work, of course). He argues that this blinds you to differences and forecloses subsequent leads that should be explored that differ from those of previous cases that might come to mind. 'One must avoid all assimilation of one case with others and one must not take off in one direction only, as one will ignore many other indicators. One has to keep an open mind' about analysing an individual case, he said.[49] According to this experienced practitioner, one should in fact *not* follow Agatha Christie's Miss Marple, who so often let the memory of an analogous configuration guide her to sleuth out the murderer . . .

Does history repeat itself?

Confirmation bias can also be found in making historical comparisons, of which historians like myself are fond. What are 'similar instances', and how similar are they? Are they 'similar' only in the mind of the superficial observer, as further study might point to decisive differences? One example worth discussing in some detail is that of seeing Stalin as acting like Hitler's twin from 1939 until the final stages of the Second World War, and as likely to be set on further expansionism after 1945.

Some form of clash between the Soviet Union – set on a strategy of spreading communism to the rest of the world, driven by faith in Marx's historical inevitability – and the western democracies-cum-market economies was inevitable also after the Second World War had seen them fight Nazi Germany together. But assuming that Stalin – who was more cautious even as this basic clash of interests became apparent, and who by the end of the Second World War was more impressed by America than Hitler had been back in 1941 – was a simple clone of Hitler was unhelpful. It certainly made the onset of the Cold War – or perhaps one should think of it as a *return* to the strife between worldwide communism and the 'capitalist' states of the 1920s and 1930s – more dangerous, more prone to turn into a Third World War. Fortunately, the danger was recognized by both sides, by Stalin earlier than by the Truman and Eisenhower administrations: already in 1946, Stalin commented on America's awe-inspiring might.[50] The Hitler–Stalin analogy made in western minds arguably led to a premature and later excessively military 'securitization' of the East–West relationship.

Hitler had expanded his Third Reich by 'salami' tactics, increasing the territory slice by slice – first marching into the demilitarized Rhineland, then annexing Austria, then demanding the Sudetenland, a region of Czechoslovakia, then in a lightning operation occupying the rest of Czechoslovakia, and then turning his attention to Poland. At the core of the Hitler–Stalin analogy was the belief that Stalin had previously proceeded and would continue to proceed in the same manner.

84 Our Biases

Colluding with Hitler, Stalin had indeed acted very similarly during the Second World War. Soviet forces had occupied half of Poland in late 1939, then the Baltic states, and then invaded Finland. Germany attacked the USSR in mid-1941, but once German aggression had been turned back on the outskirts of Moscow and in Stalingrad in 1943, the Red Army had occupied all the lands between the USSR, Berlin and Vienna. Yet, after VE Day on 8 May 1945 (9 May Moscow time), Stalin had in fact changed his approach. Indeed, he seems to have respected most of the points agreed between him and Winston Churchill in the aforementioned 'percentages agreement' of October 1944. And yet it was assumed by American and British intelligence analysts that any communist expansionist and subversive strategies adopted anywhere in the world were due to Stalin's orders.[51] In reality, some developments escaped Stalin's control entirely, as we have already seen (see Box 1.2 on the Tito–Stalin Quarrel of 1948, p. 25).

The gradual realization that communism was not a monolith, and that Stalin was not a Hitler Mark II in his peacetime strategy, did not prevent western defence analysts from loosely comparing a string of later autocrats – from Gamal Abdel Nasser to General Galtieri to Saddam Hussein and now Putin – with Hitler. This meant assuming that, as with Hitler, any concessions made to them would only encourage them in further expansionism. Therefore, their expansionism could not be stopped by peaceful reasoning, but only either by threatening or going to war. Were there no similarities at all? More general human vices, no doubt, were shared by all of them, from vainglory to the fear that if victorious expansion were to cease, their hold on power would wane. And a pattern can also be detected when a successful conqueror develops an appetite for further ventures, or, as my grandmother used to put it, *l'appétit vient en mangeant*. Alexander the Great, Caesar, Genghis Khan, Mehmet the Conqueror, the rulers of Spain in the early Age of Discovery, Gustavus Adolphus,

Frederick II of Prussia, Napoleon, the Japanese military regime of the 1930s, Hitler and indeed Stalin *during the Second World War*: they were all tempted to go further when the going was good. Yet there is little evidence that any of them initially had a clear list of areas they wanted to conquer, let alone that they thought they could conquer 'the world'. All of them were, to some extent, opportunists, seizing favourable configurations that presented themselves once they had achieved the more limited goal with which they embarked on their wars of conquest – whether this was avenging the Persian sacking of Athens or pacifying the Gauls or seizing the 'golden apple', Constantinople.

There can, however, be conscious emulation. Alexander wanted to be a new Achilles, and a series of modern rulers wanted to be seen as new Alexanders or Caesars, to which the many paintings and statues put up to these ancient conquerors around princely residences testify. Their success in emulating these ancient models was measured in terms of victories in battle and military conquests.

Similarly, other regimes hark back consciously to historic precedents. The return to a pseudo-Victorian posture of Britain as a global player under the successive Conservative governments of the 2010s and early 2020s is an example of this, whether or not it makes sense for a second-tier power long after it has lost its colonial empire and while its forces are clearly very much bound up in a joint effort to deter further Russian expansionism in Europe. Turkish President Erdoğan consciously harks back to the Ottoman Empire, whose ruler assumed the title of caliph, leader of the Islamic world. As a Turkish Defence Ministry spokesman put it around 2020, 'a great and strong Turkey . . . is the great sycamore under whose shadow many oppressed people seek shelter. From Gibraltar to Hejaz [Saudi Arabia], from the Balkans to Asia, all humanity longs for it.'[52] Finally, Putin allows himself to be cast as a new tsar, and, obligingly, the historical museum *Russia – My*

History at the great Moscow Exhibition Centre shows a 'List of Tsars from Rurik to Putin'.[53]

In the case of Putin, we need not look for some *return* to patterns of the Cold War. Putin is himself a *remnant* of the Cold War. Raised in the Cold War, a member of the Soviet secret service KGB (later the FSB), he is a carrier of the beliefs about Russia's mission and leadership role that was central to the Cold War, about its need for a protective buffer of surrounding states to ward off the hostility of an anti-communist, anti-Soviet and by extrapolation anti-Russian world. As one of his chief political opponents who knew him well enough, Vladimir Kara-Murza, recently released from a Russian prison, has argued, Putin's worldview never adjusted to the possibilities of peaceful coexistence and mutually beneficial exchanges and prosperity that the post-Cold War world offered.[54] Putin is not just *inspired* by the Cold War policies of his communist predecessors, but he actively revived them. He *is* a Cold Warrior, as are most of his leading generals who never adjusted to a post-Cold War environment. In this case, analogies between Putin's behaviour and that of his Soviet predecessors are not illustrations of some pattern of nature (or geopolitics) that *repeats* itself, but are a conscious revival of or even *continuity* in previous Cold War strategies towards the West, even if there is a good deal of tsarist nostalgia mixed in with it.

What, then, of the *longue durée* and national proclivities? On the one hand, one can identify patterns of institutional cultures and of cultural preferences in individual countries but, on the other hand, one must beware of assuming them to be static. 'National' cultures and institutional cultures change over time, along with the personalities of individuals who lead them and are part of them. Generational changes are just as important: Yugoslavia's leading elites under Tito, with their internationalist attitude and determination to cope with and accommodate ethnic diversity in a pan-Yugoslav framework, were clearly different in ethos and ideals from the leaders

Our Biases

87

who succeeded them in the late 1980s with their narrower ethnic/nationalist agendas. Even individuals change: many a leading politician who is in office for a long period of time can be seen to have shifted his or her approach on key issues – good examples include Ronald Reagan's attitude towards the Soviet Union, Margaret Thatcher's attitude towards America, François Mitterrand's attitude towards Germany and German reunification, and Helmut Kohl's attitude towards European integration. Regimes may change their approach: Robert Jervis found in his study of what went wrong in American intelligence assessments of 2002–3 of the likelihood of Saddam Hussein developing weapons of mass destruction that they had 'over-learned' lessons drawn from the 1991 Gulf War. In 1990–1, they had found that they had underestimated Iraq's secret research programmes on weapons of mass destruction. Therefore, in 2003, they assumed further hidden activity.[55]

My last warning should therefore be against constructing 'historical' patterns of arguing that 'the Ruritanians will always do X' or 'government crises in Zorania will always take the course of action Y or that of Z'. There is many an expert on Yugoslavia who in 1990 dismissed the possibility of a war of fission with the argument that Yugoslavia had forever teetered on the brink of disintegration, but that the odds for continued peaceful cooperation were always greater in the end. Any situation has within itself the potential for multiple developments, and it is the complexity of the specific forces acting upon each situation that will determine which of these potentialities becomes reality. A good analyst, like a good historian, can at best identify different *possible* outcomes. It is of course easiest to explain retrospectively why one and not the other came about. In order to do so, a profound understanding of cultural idiosyncrasies is vital; but even that in itself cannot pretend to be the magic formula for predicting the future – including the next decision of a complex individual like Slobodan Milošević or Saddam Hussein – with certainty. But awareness of cultural

88　　Our Biases

and ideological factors, of differences of worldviews and their implications, may allow an analyst to avoid errors of the enormity of those made by the British and French governments in dealing with Germany in the 1920s and 1930s, or in allowing the Rwandan genocide and the massacre of Srebrenica to happen under our very noses in 1994 and 1995 respectively.

Crying wolf and the puzzle of military exercises

Related is the problem posed for analysts when an event is expected more than once but then fails to occur. It discredits any source that announced it. The most famous recent example is that of the Yom Kippur War of 1973, where Israel was caught off guard precisely because previous alerts had proved false.

Box 2.4: The Yom Kippur War, 1973

Twice in 1973, Egyptian President Anwar Sadat had given orders for an Egyptian invasion of the Sinai Peninsula, held by Israel since the Six-Day War of 1967; twice someone whom the Israelis gave the codename 'Angel' had warned the Israelis of this imminent attack, and twice Sadat postponed it. On the first of these occasions, Israel had mobilized its reserves, something that comes at a high cost to the economy of a country, and something that, when it proves to have been unnecessary, erodes the population's faith in its government. When Sadat ordered the attack for a third time, Angel again warned the Israelis, but they began to distrust the reliability of their source who, it was thought, had cried 'wolf' once too often.[56] On 6 October 1973, the Israeli government was thus caught by surprise when the actual invasion of Sinai happened, along with an invasion from the north, from Syria. Prior to the Sukkot War begun by Hamas from Gaza exactly 50 years later in 2023, this was the worst intelligence failure Israel had suffered.

Our Biases

89

An attack that has thus been rehearsed several times, particularly as a military exercise that eventually can serve as a smokescreen for the real thing, will be particularly hard to identify as imminent, as Douglas Nicoll also noted.[57] This applied also in the following year to the Turkish invasion of Cyprus that the Turkish forces had been rehearsing since the late 1960s, the Argentinian invasion of the Falklands that eventually materialized in 1982 after a series of false alarms, and the Russian military exercises of the late 2010s and the early 2020s. In each case, previous exercises had made it uncertain whether, or if so when, an actual attack would occur.

Normally, exercises serve the purpose of training one's troops and new personnel on already existing equipment, new equipment, traditional SOPs, new procedures, with allies or other partners, and so on. Then there are political purposes. These may include the reassurance of friends and allies. Exercises can also be employed as tools of diplomacy, to reward a friendly power's supportive behaviour by including them, or to signal displeasure by excluding them from collective exercises, and, on the other side, to intimidate or coerce other powers and, specifically, to deter aggression on the part of potential adversaries.

Exercises can, however, also be covers for moving military personnel into critically contested areas or indeed preparing offensive operations. They can be designed as distractions from actual preparation for offensives elsewhere or as tests of the adversary's standard responses.

Of course, not every military exercise is the smokescreen for an invasion. But there is a clear tradition relating to the USSR/Russia and the USSR's Cold War (current or former) client states that have learned this trick from the USSR, although the Soviet Union originally learned it from the Germans. In the summer of 1939, the *Wehrmacht* used exercises along the Polish frontier to deploy troops that then attacked on 1 September

90   Our Biases

1939. In the following year, the *Wehrmacht* conducted an exercise, named Weserübung 1940, which disconcertingly had nothing to do with the River Weser that flows into the North Sea but prepared their invasion of Norway. In 1941, it was ostensibly exercises that took large *Wehrmacht* contingents into Poland, close to the demarcation line between German and Soviet-occupied territory. From this forward-based position, the *Wehrmacht* launched its surprise attack on the USSR on 22 June 1941.

The first Soviet adaptation of this pattern I have come across are the plans of 1951–3 to use exercises in Hungary and Bulgaria as cover for an invasion of Yugoslavia, to be spearheaded by the armies of these two satellite states, then to be backed by Red Army units that would follow if necessary.[58] They were postponed indefinitely in the light of strong American signals that Yugoslavia would be defended with their help. In the summer of 1968, however, the Šumava and Neman exercises were used to cow the new Czech liberal regime into scrapping their liberal reforms (the 'Prague Spring'), and when those were resisted, the Soviet invasion of Czechoslovakia in August that resulted in regime change in Prague was developed out of the exercises' deployment.

It looks very much as though this trick was taught at the Soviet military academies that included students from allied and client states, such as Egypt, India and Iraq. Anwar Sadat of Egypt used it very effectively in conjunction with the trick of inuring the adversary to his intentions by ordering the invasion of Israeli-held Sinai three times, but then putting it off twice, in 1973 (see Box 2.4, The Yom Kippur War, p. 88).

Then in 1980–1, the dockers' and workers' Solidarność movement in Poland was threatening communist rule. Soviet exercises were held in the region to put pressure on the movement to back down, with invasion plans readied for April 1980, then again for September 1981, but which were both times

Our Biases 91

deferred.[59] Preferring not to have the Soviets take matters in hand, in December 1981 the Polish military took over and imposed martial law.

It was another set of Soviet disciples, the Indian military, who without the knowledge of the government in the months from November 1986 to January 1987 played with fire in their Brass Tacks exercise along the Indo-Pakistani border, when both countries already owned nuclear weapons. How close this came to an Indian invasion of Pakistan with the intention of a limited land grab is unclear, but it took American intervention to bring the crisis to an end.[60] Shortly thereafter, in 1990, Saddam Hussein used an exercise to prepare his invasion of Kuwait. Iraq, of course, had been another client state of Russia, with its top military leaders trained in Moscow military academies.

The Russian government reverted to old Soviet tricks when the exercise Kavkaz was used in July 2008 to prepare a Russian invasion of Georgia, simultaneously proclaiming that a joint US–Georgian exercise was preparing an attack on Russian territory. Then in 2014, Moscow announced a comprehensive surprise combat-readiness inspection, starting 26 February 2014, to the north-east of Ukraine, which introduced a new twist: it distracted observers' attention from the infiltration of unmarked Russian military personnel into Crimea in order to annex the peninsula.

The ability to examine military build-ups allegedly explained by exercises, and to conduct spot inspections to verify their true purpose, was a key feature of the Conventional Forces in Europe Treaty of 1990 (Russia suspended its application of the treaty in 2007). Along with watching over its application, the Organization for Security and Cooperation in Europe (OSCE) had in 1990 adopted a document in Vienna to ensure the transparency of military exercises by enjoining all member-states to announce in advance exercises involving more than 10,000 personnel (fewer for naval exercises). This was updated several times, but from 2010 the Russian delegation at the OSCE in Vienna dragged its heels on any further update which was deemed necessary by most other member-states as the 10,000 personnel figure could be got around by pretending that one exercise actually constituted several unconnected parallel exercises. On 25 October 2018, I was invited to present my own concerns about the use of exercises to prepare military invasions to the member-states' representatives of the OSCE in Vienna, and the overwhelming majority, except for Russia and Belarus, voted for resumption of the work on the Vienna Document. But this continued to be blocked by Russia and Belarus: they have stated that this would be for as long as western sanctions remained in place in response to the Russian annexation of Crimea.

Thereafter, the Russians continued to make use of their by now well-rehearsed recipe. In a dazzling series of Russian exercises from 2020 until early 2022, they again sought to desensitize both Ukraine and the West to the danger of the actual invasion that began on 24 February 2022. Having said that, it was observable, at the latest by November 2021, even to outsiders without access to any secret intelligence, that Russian forces that had been moved near Ukraine for the large-scale Zapad exercise were not being demobilized as would have been expected had it only been an exercise.

Using military exercises to prepare an attack was thus a weapon in the Soviet strategic toolkit that continues to be used by Russia, one of many indicators of extreme continuity between the Soviet and Russian militaries and intelligence agencies. We find an honest admission of this in the writings of Russian Colonel A. A. Bartosh of the Moscow Languages University who explained in 2022, not long after the latest series of Russian military exercises to the east of Ukraine had prepared the 'special military operation', how exercises fit into an overall strategy of 'hybrid war' that attempts to avoid classical battles:

Our Biases 93

The strategy of hybrid war aims to exhaust the victim country and employs a large span or measures. . . . The aggressor State attacks clandestinely . . . An important element of the strategy of hybrid war is the deliberate impact on the State's military security sphere to exhaust itself with exorbitant defence expenditures by provoking local conflicts on its borders and strategically important regions, *by holding large-scale military exercises along its borders* with provocative scenarios, by deploying destabilising weapons systems, by using '5th columns' and networks of agents. The time frame of this strategy of exhaustion is one of several years.[61]

Nevertheless, a good number of western observers allowed themselves to be blinded by the Russian ploy of using exercises as *maskirovka*, and even in mid-February 2022 were in an unreasonable state of denial.

Denial

Denial is a bias shared across cultures. We try to ignore things we really don't want to happen and might see them more clearly as a distant possibility than when they are looming closely. NATO's Florence Gaub notes in her brilliant exploration about how we think about the future that just about all 'surprising' events or developments had been foretold (and indeed predicted by intelligence).[62] And yet warnings were ignored.

In the 1970s, concerns about environmental pollution were ubiquitous, soon to be followed by worries about the 'ozone hole' in the atmosphere and ensuing climate change. Yet little seems to have been done about this in the following decades, and when the subject returned in force in the early 2000s, there was much outright denial, particularly on the political right in the United States and Europe, and claims that this was all hype and hysteria and some sort of conspiracy to get governments

94 Our Biases

to espouse policies detrimental to the short-term economic and social welfare of their countries. At least nowadays such claims are relegated to the lunatic fringes of politics.

Drawing on his long career in the British intelligence services, the Home Office and the Ministry of Defence, Sir David Omand explains such denial – failure to make the right predictions from available evidence – in part by 'the human temptation to indulge in magical thinking, imagining that things will turn out as we want without any credible causal explanation of how that will come about. We do this to shield ourselves from the unwelcome truth that we may not be able to get what we want.'[63]

Denial and wishful thinking were present when up to a year before the outbreak of the Second World War, British Prime Minister Sir Neville Chamberlain, who had lost a son in the First World War, claimed that one could 'do business with Herr Hitler'. The alternative seemed too horrible to contemplate.

Nor were the Germans immunized against seeing the world as they wished, in denial about obvious realities. Hermann Göring, Hitler's arrogant and self-important chief of the German air force (the Luftwaffe), in early 1942 still denied the possibility of US fighter planes reaching Germany from bases in Britain when it was reported that one had been shot down near Aachen. 'It's simply not true', he said. 'I am an experienced fighter pilot myself. I know what's possible. And I know what isn't, too.' And to cap it all, he added, 'I officially assert that American fighter planes did not reach Aachen.'[64] (He also exclaimed that he would change his name to Meier if ever an enemy bomber could reach German soil, a name by which daring wits would later refer to him.)

We have already alluded to Stalin's failure to believe reports in early 1941 that the *Wehrmacht* was preparing to invade the USSR – a clear case of denial. Worse still, Stalin could have saved millions of lives in the Great Patriotic War had he heeded and acted upon Clausewitz's tenet, derived from

Napoleon's catastrophic campaign against Russia in 1812, that the defensive is the stronger form of war. Foolishly, and breaking with Lenin's admiration for the dead Prussian, Stalin had not only dismissed Clausewitz as bourgeois and thus inappropriate for Soviet military teaching. In the 1930s, he had also, in logical consistency with this rejection of Clausewitz's teaching, dismantled all the stay-behind structures existing in his country to mount a resistance movement behind enemy lines against an occupation force. Colonel Ilya Grigoryevich Starinov, who escaped the great purges of 1937–8 because he was fighting on the side of the Republicans in Spain at the time, and Panteleimon Kondrat'evič Ponomarenko, who witnessed the operations of the Soviet partisans during the Second World War, later recalled that the USSR had been well prepared to lead a popular uprising against an invading army at the beginning of the 1930s. By 1937 at the latest, Stalin and supporters held 'that preparing for partisan warfare on their own territory was defeatism and therefore treason against the fatherland'. As a result, all preparations ceased, weapons, ammunition and supply depots and technical equipment intended for this purpose were disbanded, as were training camps and partisan detachments that had already been set up. Most of the military officers who had been involved in preparations for partisan warfare up to that point were 'liquidated' in the course of the Great Purges.[65] In Stalin's strategic thinking, guerrilla-type resistance against foreign occupation such as Russia had practised in 1812, as recorded by General Denis Vasilevich Davidov, was incompatible with Marxist concepts of historical progress. He was thus in denial of the possibility that war might ever again take place on Russian soil.

The year 1941 was decidedly one of catastrophic misjudgements: the next one followed barely six months later, when the United States' leadership was reluctant to believe in the possibility of a surprise attack on American military installations as far away from Japan as Hawaii. Biases came to weigh heavily,

96   Our Biases

and a series of misjudgements led to the belated distribution of the relevant intelligence warnings of the imminent Japanese attack on the US fleet anchored at Pearl Harbor. And that despite a long-term, strategic concern about possible future war with Japan.

Box 2.5: Pearl Harbor – The Japanese Attack on the United States, December 1941

As early as the 1920s, US military planners had seen Japan as a potential threat to US interests in the Far East. The Second World War, caused by Japanese expansionism, had started in the Far East even before Hitler came to power in Germany, with Japan's move into Manchuria on the Asian mainland in 1931, followed by Japan's invasion of China from 1937. After France's armistice with Germany in June 1940, Japan seized French Indochina. In mid-1940, US President Franklin D. Roosevelt moved the US Pacific Fleet from San Diego in California to Hawaii. By early 1941, Roosevelt was sufficiently worried about his navy's ability to contain Japanese expansionism to contemplate giving up the Philippines in case of a Japanese invasion, yet he tried to deter such an attack by telling the Tokyo government that the United States would take action – undefined – if Japan attacked 'neighbouring countries'. In other words, hostilities between the United States and Japan had been seen as highly possible for two decades.

In July 1941, American oil exports to Japan were stopped, which instilled a sense of urgency in Tokyo: in November, the Japanese government proposed a deal whereby Japanese forces would withdraw from French Indochina if the United States resumed oil exports. Roosevelt's refusal, contained in a note from Secretary of State Cordell Hull, demanded more, namely the withdrawal from China. But even before this note was delivered, the faction in the Japanese military leadership arguing for a direct confrontation with the United States had won out in Tokyo, and a Japanese fleet including six aircraft carriers had been despatched on 26 November 1941 to attack the US fleet in Pearl Harbor, two days before deciding to terminate negotiations with American government representatives about the resumption of fuel supplies. There were intelligence indicators of a change in Japanese approach, but none anywhere near as clear as the intelligence received by the Kremlin prior to Barbarossa. Eventually, on 7 December in the late hours of the night and early in the morning, an overflight by Japanese aircraft had been identified by a radar site at Opana on Oahu, Hawaii, and Japanese submarines had been spotted near the access to Pearl Harbor, but attempts to track them had proved unsuccessful.[66]

The attack itself began on 7 December 1941 just before 8 o'clock in the morning, Hawaiian time, with a bombardment of US warships anchored in Pearl Harbor. Japan's declaration of war followed later the same day. The Japanese military falsely assumed that this loss of naval vessels would simply paralyse the United States, rather than catalyse determination to avenge the attack and defeat Japan utterly. Japan's operational success ultimately proved a disastrous strategic miscalculation.

Similarly, in the Cold War, early (long-term) predictions as to when the USSR would be able to field an atom and then an H-bomb arsenal were fairly realistic, but the actual Soviet tests were greeted with surprise and consternation among western leaders, not to mention the media. There seems to be a pattern that something may more easily be seen as possible or likely if it is still some time in the future than if it is imminent, when denial sets in.

After the end of the Cold War with the collapse of communist rule throughout Eastern Europe between late 1989 and early 1991, that post-Soviet Russia might turn bad was seen as an imminent possibility. Consider the prophetic words written

98 Our Biases

in 1993 by the astute American defence analyst David S. Yost. He asked,

> what approach will Moscow adopt towards its former dominions? . . . will the Russians pursue harsh Realist . . . policies, seeking to dominate several, if not all, of their weaker neighbours or even to incorporate them into a new empire or sphere of influence? Might the Russians even attempt to devise a new quasi-Revolutionist ideology to furnish a legitimacy principle for such an empire? In view of Russia's past and the discrediting of Marxism-Leninism, this might be an anti-western messianic ideology, driven by a determination to maintain Russia's great power status, perhaps with strands of authoritarianism, Russian national chauvinism, Orthodoxy, and/or pan-Slavism.[67]

There were others at the time to whom similar thoughts occurred. Comparisons were made even in the early 1990s between post-communist Russia and its potential future and defeated Germany in its democratic incarnation of the Weimar Republic that then gave way to Hitler's dictatorship.

Yet relations seemed cautiously friendly as the 1990s went on. Even the first years of Putin's rule, between mid-1999 and 2007, seemed to indicate that he was open to a cooperative relationship with other states and organizations, including NATO and the EU, and exchanges flourished. Putin spoke about Russia finding her place in Europe, noting that 'In terms of spirit and culture, Russia is an integral part of European civilisation.'[68] Many then refused to heed the message of his speech at the Munich Security Conference in February 2007 that his mind had turned to a more confrontational approach, and many, including myself, tried to ignore the implications of the Russo-Georgian War that resulted in a successful Russian land grab. Then in 2014, Russia annexed Crimea by very clever moves, infiltrated Russian and mercenary forces into the Eastern Ukrainian regions of Luhansk and Donetsk, and

Our Biases

then organized a referendum in Crimea under Russian military occupation that, unsurprisingly, produced the result that a majority of inhabitants wanted to belong to Russia. When no further major moves ensued for several years thereafter, many of us thought, or rather hoped, that Putin had now achieved his aims and would not have any further territorial ambitions. People in the West really, really did not want further confrontation – French President Emmanuel Macron even talked about a reboot of relations and considered relaxing the sanctions imposed after the Crimean annexation. The West had no interest in returning to the Cold War, with the fear but also the expenses and arms race that might entail. The world had enough on its plate with the enormous task of mitigating climate change, and then there were the long-term effects of the 2008 financial crisis (with growing support for populist parties in many democracies) and then of Covid-19 to worry about. All good opportunities for Putin to exploit the West's other preoccupations.

Denial is also an irrational approach to the moral dilemma posed by nuclear weapons. The dilemma might be summarized thus: if nuclear war occurred, it could well exterminate human life in large parts of the world, or perhaps, through the spread of radioactivity, of the whole world. If nuclear weapons are removed from all arsenals, however, this would make a recurrence of conventional wars up to and beyond the scale of destruction and death of the Second World War possible. We want neither. Nuclear strategists hope that they could make such large-scale war unthinkable through credible propositions of how they might, if deterrence broke down, use nuclear weapons to restore deterrence in ways short of bringing on all-out nuclear war.

There is no dispute that the destructive power of nuclear weapons is horrific, or that a world in which no weapons were needed because no one ever thought of going to war would be ideal. The disagreement concerns whether in the

100 Our Biases

absence of such an ideal world, with such ideal pacific humans, nuclear weapons – by their very existence or with limited use to restore deterrence – provide a barrier to conflicts escalating to something like the Second World War. Indeed, nuclear strategists hope that some wars would not even be initiated. Disarmers, however, have no confidence that such nuclear use could be limited or that the complex signalling that surrounds deterrence could be controlled to produce an acceptable nonescalatory outcome.

Denial, however, comes in where disarmers call for the banning of nuclear weapons but refuse to propose alternatives. There are two elements to this. One is the disarmers' general failure to address the extreme fragility of arms control regimes in the absence of an enforcement mechanism (an impartial world judge and police force that would step in and compel a state in breach of such a treaty to surrender the weapons, with the state meekly complying rather than using those very weapons to tell the world police to get lost). We can observe this now in the case of Iran which is a signatory to the Non-Proliferation Treaty but over the years under the mullahs has been edging towards becoming a nuclear weapons-owning state. Sanctions imposed by other Treaty signatories have not stopped this.

Notwithstanding their signing of the Biological Weapons Convention of 1972, the Soviet Union continued to work on its offensive biological weapons programme[69] and its continuing offensive chemical weapons programme, again despite Russia having signed up to the Chemical Weapons Convention of 1997. The former was last brought to the world's attention with the Novichok poison attacks, some successful, some thwarted, on Russian defectors or political opponents of Putin. The other part of disarmers' denial is the widespread refusal to think through how, in a world without nuclear weapons, one could deter bellicose powers from starting anything that might become major war. (Not all disarmers have failed to

Our Biases 101

confront this issue. In the 1980s, the Lansbury House Trust and the Bradford School of Peace Studies set up a commission under the chairmanship of Frank Blackaby to study alternatives to nuclear deterrence. The only alternative they could see, presented in their findings of 1983, was a massive increase in conventional forces.[70])

Boiled frogs and grey rhinos

Notoriously, analysts (myself included) display a blindness to change once they have concluded their examination of a situation or a government's posture or a leader's worldview, and think they now know enough about it. This is a sub-category of confirmation bias, one that makes analysts reluctant to look for and notice change. Heraclitus' observation that one never steps into the same river twice contends against the conviction, developed especially by country specialists, that a year or longer spent in a particular country makes them understand it and enables them to pontificate authoritatively about almost all aspects of it, including a government that comes into power after they have left or subsequent shifts in public opinion. For a while, this may hold, but already the next government will likely include ministers the analysts did not know about and policies they did not anticipate, even when following news media assiduously. Reluctant to relinquish their reputations as experts, analysts are biased to claim expertise when in reality it is waning.

Gradual change is less noticeable than sudden change, and in this context the urban myth is often invoked that a frog thrown into boiling water will try to make its escape, but if it sits in water that is gradually heated, it will not notice the danger until too late and will die. (Actually, the frog will die of scalding in the first scenario, but let us leave that aside.) The problem of gradual change is that one can live in the hope that it can be stopped and reversed, and one might realize too

102 Our Biases

late that the point of no return has passed. This may well also apply to dealing with a dictatorial regime that turns increasingly aggressive while simultaneously strengthening its grip on its own population and putting opposition into prisons or camps, or administering a little Novichok poison to particularly prominent opponents every now and then. And even when it is well recognized that a regime is undemocratic, oppressing its own population but stopping short of genocide, international law postulates that other states should keep out of this regime's domestic affairs. Even the superpower the United States, along with its less powerful allies, has conceded, in the batch of national and alliance security strategies produced in 2022–3, that they have little choice but to cooperate with states that do not share democratic values. If at least they are willing to uphold international law, they are in American parlance now referred to as 'countries that subscribe to the rules-based international order', leaving aside whether they share other values such as human rights or democracy.[71] This realpolitik approach befits second-tier and declining powers but increases tolerance of and analytical blindness to regimes that are steadily sliding towards tyranny.

The problem of diagnosing gradual change is also one affecting regular foreign policy or intelligence reports, where small events or trends illustrating such change may either go unreported altogether or be reported without much emphasis (think of an example such as 'there are unverified reports that the garrisons in X and in Y are to be strengthened', which at best will lead to non-urgent requests for further research). Venturing a guess as to whether small changes form part of a larger pattern, and where they might lead, is risky, and thus it is harder to choose to report than to report clear-cut measures (such as 'By decree, the army will be doubled in size this summer'). Roberta Wohlstetter's magisterial work on intelligence and decision-making failure in December 1941 commented that the lack of impact in Washington of the alerts issued prior to the attacks

Our Biases 103

on Pearl Harbor was due in part to their formulations. They said in effect, 'Something is brewing', or 'Get ready for a surprise move in any direction – maybe.' Phrases characterizing contingencies as 'possible' or 'strongly possible' or saying that they 'cannot be entirely ruled out' or are 'unpredictable' do not guide decisions with a very sure hand.[72]

This leads us to grey rhinos, 'a well-known and slow-moving risk that can cause or amplify . . . crises, if it's ignored long enough', in the definition of Marja Nykänen, Deputy Governor of the Bank of Finland.[73] European governments' under-investment in defence and failure to upkeep and renew munitions stocks in recent years is such an example in the context of the Russia–Ukraine War. The very fact that one has identified such a risk but that it has failed to have an immediate impact makes one complacent to it – until it storms out of the bush and tramples everything underfoot.

Regular reporting fatigue

Change at a slow, incremental pace is difficult to capture. This is not the only problem with regular reporting. How is reporting institutionalized? Think it through bureaucratically. Sometime back when what we call the Middle Ages turned into 'modern' times in Europe, ministers advising their city councils on matters of security sooner or later found that they could not keep track of every development abroad all by themselves and commissioned others to report to them on anything of importance without being asked to do so each time, or to identify new lines of inquiry. Thus city-states like Venice or Bruges that traded widely put into place systems of collecting information about what was going on elsewhere that could touch on their trading interests. Larger polities followed suit; famously, under Queen Elizabeth I and her chief minister Robert Cecil, Francis Walsingham was charged with setting up agents on the European mainland. Other ministers, like Robert

104 Our Biases

Devereux, Earl of Essex, had their own network of informants. Of course, those were paid in return for their services.

If reports came in irregularly, perhaps with long pauses, then a minister commissioning them might wonder whether the agent was just happily spending the money earned rather than chasing after new intelligence. Ministers would thus encourage regular reporting. But the more regularly that intelligence reports come in, the less outstandingly important the matters they cover (so as to have something to say every time) and the less attention they are paid. Except in times of crisis, regular news updates by themselves get less attention than irregular ones. A later inquiry into how advance intelligence on attacks in New York and Washington on 11 September 2001 did not spark preventive executive action established the following: information passed by the US Intelligence Services to US President George Bush Jr on 6 August 2001 on Al Qaeda's planned action on US soil (heading: 'Bin Ladin Determined to Strike in US'), noting that something was about to happen, did not register with the president. It was the 36th such report that year on Al Qaeda, and as it was not discussed with the president afterwards, he only dimly remembered it.[74] On a more mundane level, something similar applies to, for example, the subscriptions academics take out for journals – when these arrive regularly, they pile up on desks, unread or at best skimmed through, given the boring regularity of their arrival. It may take an external prompt to go back to them to spot a bit of information of considerable relevance to us in an issue of the journal buried under many others, along with essays to mark, book manuscripts and unpublished articles to review, and so on.

When something of exceptional importance does happen, the 24-hour television news cycle now gives many decision makers a lazy excuse for waiting until more information is brought to them, rather than asking their staff for more information about the actors, the background or the historical context. Lazy journalists also fail to provide this, favouring instead comments by the man or woman in the street that may or may not be representative of public opinion, and certainly throw no light on the wider background. This takes us to the question of what analysts (and decision makers) know and what they do not, but should, know.

Overconfidence or optimism bias

Biases in conflictual situations, it is often commented, include either seeing the enemy as 10 feet tall or as utterly inferior, and then being taken by surprise when the latter is not the case. Colonialists in fighting down rebellions or attacks on their trade or settlements or armed forces overseas often found that the Indigenous forces they were dealing with may not have been as well armed but devised many ways of mitigating this asymmetry. Overconfidence in their own means and ways would contribute to initial convictions on the part of colonialists that the Indigenous forces would be easy to deal with. Overconfidence – also referred to as optimism bias – has been identified as a key cause of British failure when attempting to protect Norway from German invasion and occupation in late 1940, along with other perennial flaws in British strategy making, directly linked to an underestimation of the enemy.[75] The underestimation of the ability and perseverance of hostile Afghan groups to resist, given the social and geographic characteristics of Afghanistan, was shared by Britons, Soviets and NATO member-state governments in their respective invasions of Afghanistan in the nineteenth to twenty-first centuries. Unsurprisingly, therefore, 'optimism bias' features repeatedly in the report of the British House of Commons Defence Committee on the reasons for (British, but one could widen it to western) failure in Afghanistan that ended in the collapse, in a flash, of 18 years of western intervention.[76] Only half a year later, in February 2022, Russian President Putin, for one, seems to have thought that Ukraine would be a pushover when believing a blitzkrieg against Ukraine would succeed.

When adversaries then respond in unconventional ways, or by exploiting asymmetries and the colonialists' rigidity and inflexibility, their standard operational procedures and well-rehearsed tactics, they are quickly accused of not playing by the book. The link is quickly made with 'sneaky oriental ways' of using ambushes, surprise and other stratagems, contrasted with a frank and honest 'western way of war' of seeking a frontal battle on open ground. This is a trope that goes back to a contrasting of Greek and Persian ways of fighting supposedly made by a Persian general during the Persian Wars with Greece in the fifth century BC. It was picked up by an American classicist who in the late twentieth century tried to fit a 'western way of war' into the Procrustean bed of such open confrontation, facilitated by superior weaponry and especially firepower.[77] (As many critics have since pointed out, the 'West' is not above using all the means attributed to their 'wily' enemies when it suits.)

Overconfidence in one's own abilities can also result from believing in one's own propaganda. Such overconfidence has been identified on all sides at the outbreak of the First World War, when each expected a quick victory, a war that would be 'over by Christmas'. It was present in both the German and the Soviet sides in 1941 when Hitler's *Wehrmacht* attacked the Soviet Union. The underestimation of the ability and perseverance of hostile Afghan groups to resist, in the social and geographic context of that country, was shared by Britons, Soviets and Americans in their respective invasions of Afghanistan in the nineteenth to twenty-first centuries. Optimism bias can be found on the Soviet side when Khrushchev decided to place nuclear weapons in Cuba, and on the American side when the United States intervened in Vietnam in the 1960s, and when it attacked Iraq in 2003.[78]

Putin's overconfidence bias of February 2022 has already been noted.

* * *

To sum up: however smart some of us may be, we are ourselves less than 'rational' in the sense of consequently and coherently making decisions that promote our overall best interests. Our actions deviate from these goals under the influence of secondary interests, of temptations and emotional overreactions, of petty personal agendas and grudges that can seriously endanger the pursuit of our primary goals.

We have not yet exhausted the list of biases which we are prone to use in our own thinking. We also act on insufficient knowledge; we make dangerous guesses and construct flawed narratives out of scraps of evidence, ignoring evidence that does not fit our preferred narratives.

In the following, we shall focus on a number of biases that are more complex, that are to do with our assumptions about knowledge and the way we think we can use what we know.

3

Knowns and Unknowns (and How We Use Them)

What do we know, what don't we know, what can we know? There are multiple fallacies surrounding the knowledge of what one can know, the most important of which is obviously that of thinking one can know everything. But can one ever know enough to take big decisions? Or can one be so swamped by knowledge that one cannot see the wood for the trees?

Too little or too much knowledge

When I was an undergraduate studying history, I was an unbearable swot. If a book or an article was on my reading list, I would read it. I would walk to the ends of London to find it in some library, not always easy: the timetable for teaching history modules throughout the huge University of London with its many colleges meant that, in any one week, there would easily be a hundred of us all chasing far fewer copies of Livy's *Ab urbe condita* or Gregory of Tours' *History of the Franks*. And yet I was amazed to find that fellow students of mine often produced much better essays than me, essays not only of greater stylistic merit but also of greater clarity and simplicity,

Knowns and Unknowns 109

having read much less. I finally found an answer, aside from inferior or superior skills: they wrote better *because* they had read less. Especially if among the few things they *had* read, there were those key articles or books containing (or, even better, summarizing) the key debates on the subject at hand. Meanwhile, I found it hard to see the wood, losing my way among all the trees, as my essays got longer and longer and less and less focused on one central argument which tutors so liked.

Daniel Kahneman explains this in much simpler and more generalizable terms. He calls this the 'story bias', and he describes the simple and oh-so-persuasive answer as the fallacy of thinking that the information you have ('what you see') 'is all there is'. We construct narratives based on the knowledge we have, and often less knowledge lends itself better to being transformed into narratives that make sense to us than more knowledge, which might include contradictory facts. Many a good storyline would break down if we had more knowledge. This is why, to the layman, a historical novel is often more satisfactory than a historiography based on all the evidence available. The novel allows the novelist to create coherent characters, with no need to explain away contradictions or decisions which are not in character. Kahneman warns that in a real-life situation, where analysts must make responsible decisions, they will be tempted to make do with the information they have, constructing narratives that look persuasive, when they should have gone out to gather more information.[1] Or, as John Maynard Keynes quipped, 'There is nothing a government hates more than to be well-informed; for it makes the process of arriving at decisions much more complicated.'[2]

Indeed, international politics 'imposes heavy information processing demands on policy makers' who have a finite capacity for doing so and adopt 'simplifying strategies' to cope. Decision makers use shortcuts to digest and interpret incoming information. Instead of evaluating each piece of news in its

110 Knowns and Unknowns

own particular contexts, as we have discussed, they use historical analogies, 'cognitive maps, operational codes, ... schemas', 'scripts' or narratives germane to their particular culture to interpret the information.[3]

There is a flip side to the realization that one should avoid shortcuts and find out more about each particular piece of news. Rolf Dobelli, with his manifold insights into the business world, economics, journalism and think tanks, warns of thinking you always need more information, and then even more, before you can come to a decision. First, some decisions cannot wait; second, huge amounts of data gathered may be irrelevant or may shed only marginally more light on the problem at hand; and third, too much detail may get us lost among the trees and unable to see the contours of the forest.[4] Moreover, decisions are often time sensitive. A mass of material that is just repetitive might not help us get closer to a good decision. Quantity does not necessarily mean quality, and the crucial piece of information that helps us understand what is going on may still be missing (or may be the needle buried in the haystack). The structural problem is that we won't know that a stack of new articles and books on whatever it is we are concerned about is not bringing anything new to the table unless we have read them all – with minds open to the possibility that a crucial new factor is hiding under a word or formulation that no 'wordsearch' software would associate with what we are looking for.

Related to the propensities of either telling gratifying (if unrealistic) stories on the basis of too little evidence, or drowning oneself in too much, is the problem of differentiating between superficial knowledge and expert knowledge. The great guru's assistant may have heard her lecture on her great subject of expertise with which she tours the universities and think tanks a sufficient number of times to be able to give it in her stead. Nevertheless, the assistant won't have the research-based knowledge to back up the statements made,

Knowns and Unknowns

and is unlikely to bring up additional evidence when the questions come. Or another example, out of the blue can appear a charismatic self-proclaimed expert who puts things so simply and persuasively that s/he advances to being special adviser for some problem or other. Meanwhile, long-standing experts with all their detailed knowledge of the issue in all its complexity stand around wondering how this person got the ear of those in power, spouting superficial stuff, putting forward unrealistic panacea solutions, but doing so very eloquently. Detailed knowledge does not always go along with eloquence, yet time-pressed decision makers are more likely to listen to those who can put things succinctly, with neat proposals for action – an understandable bias, but not necessarily the best.

Unknown unknowns

Related to whether one knows too much or too little is the problem of unknown unknowns. US Defense Secretary Donald Rumsfeld became famous for some of his idiosyncratic public statements, some of which he was derided for unjustly. This latter category included the remarkably insightful comment that there were four categories of knowledge of key importance for decision makers: the things they knew (known knowns), the things they knew they did not know but might ask their staff or the intelligence services to research (the known unknowns), the things they didn't know they knew (unknown knowns), which might be relevant information that was slumbering somewhere in a drawer or had been gathered but never evaluated or passed on; and finally, unknown unknowns, that is, things they did not realize they needed to know.

What one needs to know could be anything from the significance of movements of particular raw materials or machine components needed to build specific machines or weapons systems, or the gradual transformation of a key export commodity – think of Russian grain – into a strategic tool of coercion to

112   Knowns and Unknowns

– most difficult to track – what is going on in the hearts and minds of key leaders of another nation, another culture. The latter is not only a matter of personal mentality but also culture specific, and often the most elusive for generalists who know little or nothing about the particular biographies of the leaders, the ideational and cultural context and the historical experiences that have marked that culture. Aggressive schemes, nurtured by and flourishing in collective national mentalities valuing glory and military prowess and harbouring grudges, can have their seeds in some dark and unexpected corner of a society. This can be in a future leader's time in jail – where Adolf Hitler penned *Mein Kampf* – or in some perceived collective humiliation, revived in the rhetoric of populist parties years after the event; or in some publication, like Jean-Jacques Rousseau's *Social Contract*, Oswald Spengler's *Demise of the West* or Aleksandr Dugin's *Foundations of Geopolitics*, that touches a particular culture's nerve or 'soul' in a context of crisis and political-ethical disorientation.[5] Only a reflexive observer, deeply immersed in that culture, might recognize the beginning of a sea change.[6]

One of the weaknesses of most governments' foreign affairs and intelligence analysis agencies is that they are perpetually overstretched and cannot employ specialists for every country of the world. In prioritizing where treasure and staff are to be deployed, difficult choices have to be made. For example, in 1991, the British Foreign Office's Planning Staff, presented with the choice of devoting resources to the possibility that the Soviet Union, a nuclear weapons-owning state, would implode in a civil war or to that of Yugoslavia falling apart, the former was chosen, the latter happened. This may mean, however, that some unmonitored and thus unexpected development in a faraway country about which we know too little blows up in our faces.

Known unknowns difficult to uncover are hidden not just in the realm of capabilities (did Saddam Hussein have, or is Iran

Knowns and Unknowns

currently developing, weapons of mass destruction?). Known unknowns are often what goes on in the minds of other decision makers. And time and again, inducing what they might be thinking from how we would think if we were in their shoes (see mirror imaging above) is not helpful. How does one realize, however, that there are emotional and ideational forces at play that might override material capabilities? That brush aside considerations that it would be premature to launch a military operation when a force build-up is not completed, or when certain weapons systems have not yet arrived, or oil prices are disadvantageous to the enterprise? Trying to get into the minds of adversaries and of other parties whom one had not suspected of suddenly creating a problem for the world in general and us in particular, like the Argentine government on the eve of the Falklands War, requires what anthropologists call 'deep immersion'. This means real understanding, ideally some analytically minded and articulate observer living in the country over a long period of time, rather than desk officers rotating every two years and reading only the most 'relevant' intelligence documents translated into English (because they do not read any of the languages spoken in the set of countries they need to monitor). The Franks Report on British intelligence and foreign-policy analysis failure regarding Argentine intentions pointed to articles that had appeared in the Argentine press that were not taken sufficiently seriously by British analysts – something as simple as that.[7] Monitoring this is of course one of the jobs of an embassy, indicating that, as the parliamentary committee chaired by Lord Franks suggested, there was insufficient concertedness between the Foreign and Commonwealth Office and the Ministry of Defence or, we might add, that reports were not heeded due to regular reporting fatigue, and/or the unrecognized slow deterioration (the boiled frog syndrome). Either way, the Franks Committee was, diplomatically put, 'not sure that at all important times the assessments staff were fully aware of the weight of the

114   Knowns and Unknowns

Argentine press campaign in 1982'.[8] Similarly, Robert Jervis thought the CIA in the Carter administration would have done a better job predicting the Iranian Islamic Revolution of 1979 if it had followed the Iranian press and had had more indigenous agents in Iran who could have gauged public opinion from barber shop and taxi conversations, mixing with the people (see also Box 3.1, p. 128). There is also a bias highlighted in both admonitions, namely the bias of organizations paying more attention and credence to reports with 'top secret' stamped on them than to reporting based on open sources.

Not knowing which question to ask – the unknown unknowns – incidentally is one of the problems of the famous 'intelligence cycle', which puts the decision maker's question addressed to the intelligence services at the top. It is always difficult in such a system for experts to make themselves heard to explain that different questions should be asked. This is a structural problem with all bureaucratic politics: the difficulty of feeding any question and matter of concern, any advice or observations, into decision-making cycles when they are at a point where the initial tasking has passed.

Among unknown unknowns is also the unknown trigger problem. There might have been a single (or set of) report(s) or info that triggered an overreaction. A notable example of the former dates from the American Civil War. It is the accidental loss by a Confederation courier and recovery by Union soldiers of Robert E. Lee's Special Order #191, which outlined his entire campaign plan for the Maryland Campaign after his army had reached Frederick in early September 1862.[9] An equally notable example is the false report of a planned German attack on the Netherlands in the spring of 1939, which German *Abwehr* (counter-espionage) officers, critical of Hitler's plans, conveyed to London. Although the attack did not materialize, further reports pointed to Poland as Germany's most likely next victim. Coming on the heels of the Dutch invasion scare, this finally tipped the postures of the Chamberlain and Daladier

Knowns and Unknowns

governments in London and Paris respectively, and led to the United Kingdom's and France's guarantee for Poland.[10] These were unknown unknowns for the respective adversaries.

Herd behaviour and group think

Herds of animals pick up on each other's feelings and fears. They can be incited by individual animals to become alert and frightened, with dogs barking, geese honking or monkeys chattering excitedly and, if they are cattle or sheep, to take to flight, to stampede and even inadvertently to propel themselves over a cliff en masse. Humans are not so different, as stock market behaviour illustrates.

Irving Janis, an eminent psychologist at Yale University, made extremely important breaches in the defences of the rational actor assumption in IR theories. One in particular was achieved by showing that groups of decision makers often converge in their views – analyses of a situation or prescriptions for action – to the detriment of considering alternatives that deserve consideration. He called this 'group think'.[11] He underscored collective deliberations when a group of people eschews debate among themselves by embracing a single opinion, or those in which a single individual, perhaps with the power of agenda setting, manages to steer a group to his or her preferred conclusion. This also subsumes what psychologists have called the 'bandwagon effect' in following the views of a group or an articulate leader.

A different sort of group think can emerge when several individuals, sometimes at different ends of the world, have read the same things and have been educated with the same case studies. In the 1990s, I came up with a number of thoughts about the evolving situation in Europe, drawing analogies with previous historical events I had studied. Almost invariably, I would soon thereafter see articles that the Johns Hopkins and Harvard-educated German journalist Josef Joffe had just published in *Die Süddeutsche Zeitung*, one of the major German newspapers. Clearly, we had both immersed ourselves at some stage in the international history of the twentieth century and kept seeing parallels with earlier configurations. Nor were we alone, as it turned out: comparisons between post-communist Russia and the Weimar Republic were made by other observers as well.

This in itself is not an irrational bias, but when you have a group of decision makers all with the same analogies in mind, the same experiences, the same cultural background, the same values, group think can emerge, excluding alternative interpretations of reality, squeezing out alternative reactions to events. A glaring example of this was Israel's security community's thinking in the days before the Yom Kippur War. Group think was at work when in October 1973 the Israeli defence establishment dismissed the likelihood of an Egyptian-cum-Syrian attack. Group think among their successors was at work in October 2023, when incoming intelligence about unusual Hamas activities was received. Group think, combined with other biases such as denial, can be very dangerous.

Group think prevailed in parts of the United States and British governments in late 2002 and early 2003 with regard to the supposed danger posed by Iraq and the need to launch a preventive attack to stop it from developing weapons of mass destruction (see Box 1.4 on Curveball, p. 47). Group think was present also in NATO in the 1990s and early 2000s when the elephant in the room was Russia: everyone was concerned to keep NATO alive lest the honeymoon with Russia did not last and Russia turned bad again, yet no one wanted to say so lest this proved a self-fulfilling prophecy. At the same time, I can witness to the fact that there was unease, even among NATO staff, about what would turn out to be the first wave of admissions of former Warsaw Pact members to NATO. Did this latent fear of what the future might hold prepare the ground for a new Cold War that we can now, with hindsight, say began

Knowns and Unknowns

117

around 2007 or 2008? Yet NATO did not act on its collective fears of losing Russia at the time. Comprehensive defence planning for an attack on the Alliance had ceased and to my knowledge only resumed after 24 February 2022. Still, given the fears of the Baltic States, which had been under Moscow's direct rule as Soviet republics, and the Eastern European states that had had experience of Soviet forces stationed on their soil, it is understandable that they wanted to hedge against all eventualities by seeking shelter under the wing of big mother hen NATO.

In hindsight – yet another bias – we edit memories of our own views to claim we had predicted things in the past when we actually sat on the fence, saw several possible outcomes or felt ambiguously about them at the time. When we are caught in any given international crisis, what we see is usually far less clear, far messier, than appears in hindsight when we know what events led to. It is generally only later that we realize that certain events ushered in or were the first stage of particular developments, what parts of a confused picture made sense, what parts were irrelevant, chaff, unrelated or coincided accidentally with others.

Methodological fallacies

Theory is central to most literature produced in recent years in the field of IR. As Colin and Miriam Elman summed it up, most scholars of IR are interested in (past) events only as cases used 'to generate, test, or refine theory.'[12] For practitioners, however, a theory in need of adaptation (refinement) every time it is tested against a new case is not greatly helpful. As Richard Lepgold put it cogently, 'Theory offers little explanatory power if it must be re-invented each time issues, actors, and eras change'.[13] Nor is the Popperian binary of 'this theory is true/is false' always helpful for practitioners. Something may

118   Knowns and Unknowns

seem 'true' one day, when until then *n* cases have occurred all showing a particular pattern, and 'false' the next, when the *n* + 1st case deviates from the pattern.

There are fallacies that are particular to certain methodologies of researching the policies of individual governments and other parties to international relations. Let us look at three, each related to a branch of the discipline of International Relations. Theoreticians' focus on individual branches blinkers both themselves and their students to the possibility that it fails entirely to approach the subject from an angle appropriate to it, an angle that will only emerge if one engages with the subject deeply, on its own terms and without theoretical prejudices.

Trusting poultry: Russell's chicken and Taleb's turkey

The first is that of statistics and their (in)applicability to predictions. In his *Problems of Philosophy*, the twentieth-century philosopher Bertrand Russell discussed that of 'induction', the inference of a general law or rule from particular instances. Already in the Age of Enlightenment, his Scottish predecessor David Hume had questioned the logic of postulating that the sun would rise tomorrow from the observation that it had done so for every previous morning one had lived and seen it do so. That example stretches the willingness of any reader to share his scepticism. Bertrand Russell made Hume's case somewhat more plausible by highlighting the fallacy to assume that because some particular event has been systematically recurrent in our experience, it will recur the next time: 'Food that has a certain appearance generally has a certain taste,' he wrote, and therefore 'it is a severe shock to our expectations when the familiar appearance is found to be associated with an unusual taste.' He remarked that animals were also prone to this fallacy, so that 'A horse which has been often driven along a certain road resists the attempt to drive him in a different

Knowns and Unknowns

direction. Domestic animals expect food when they see the person who feeds them.' Thus a chicken will become trusting of the farmer who has fed it every day. When on one day, let's call it the n + 1st day, the farmer 'at last wrings its neck instead', this shows 'that more refined views as to the uniformity of nature would have been useful to the chicken'.[14] Substituting a turkey for the chicken to please an American readership, this example has gained renewed fame in the writings of Nasim Nicholas Taleb in his very successful demolition job with regard to statistics-based probabilities and improbabilities.[15] Then there is the opposite assumption, namely, that something cannot exist or happen because we have never seen it before. The title of Taleb's book in question – *The Black Swan* – refers to the assumption made over two millennia in Europe that swans could only be white, a notion that made its way into philosophical debates as a statement of the obvious and of what could be ruled out, until black swans were discovered in Australia.

I was utterly guilty of such an assumption with my little but insufficient knowledge of Yugoslavia back in 1990–1. This federal state had only come into being as a single state in the interwar period, and under Josip Broz Tito's rule it had encountered several crises in which its component states wanted more autonomy. At least two of these began in Kosovo. Each time, the crisis was resolved by some constitutional reform. After Tito's death, tensions had increased, and as the Cold War came to an end with communism – the bond that had held this multi-ethnic federation together – discredited in Europe, fission became imminent. I shrugged off predictions that the country would disintegrate into civil war with the argument that each past crisis had been contained, and so would the next . . . and of course, I could not have been more mistaken.

The n + 1 fallacy is also found elsewhere. In a study published in 2017, Bruno Tertrais, an otherwise extremely astute and insightful commentator on defence issues, expressed his belief that the nuclear taboo will continue to hold and that no accidents or misunderstandings, let alone deliberate nuclear use, pose substantial threats to the world. He deduced this from the past history of roughly thirty-seven 'close calls' – crises involving nuclear weapons – as not one of them led to actual war.[16] He argued with possibly unwarranted optimism that safety measures will continue to prevent technical accidents but, even if they occurred, they would not be misunderstood as nuclear use by the other side, as all sides would handle anything nuclear with the caution it deserves. The optimism of Tertrais's argument has been countered by Benoît Pelopidas, who points out that it is extremely worrying that despite all the effort put into nuclear safety and security, there *have* been at least thirty-seven incidents (probably several more were successfully hushed up), many of which did not turn into catastrophes by pure luck. In one case, the wind turned just in time to stop a fire from spreading to aircraft with nuclear weapons on board; in another, a safety system just escaped deactivation by a millimetre. Moreover, what of a technical accident occurring in times of crisis?[17] Imagine a nuclear explosion accidentally occurring in the context of the Russian war against Ukraine: might this lead to a nuclear riposte?

The difference in judgement between Tertrais and Pelopidas boils down to the former believing that there would be rational actors on both sides of the crisis, so that accidental misunderstandings can be managed, while Pelopidas, for many of the reasons given above, remains sceptical that common sense as *we* define it would always prevail over standard operational procedures. Famously, Soviet Colonel Stanislav Petrov on 26 September 1983 ignored his launch-on-warning instructions when he (rightly) surmised that a technical warning of incoming enemy missiles must be due to technical failure in the Soviet radar system. Yet had somebody else been on duty that night with more faith in Soviet technology, the latter

Knowns and Unknowns 121

might still have executed the launch-on-warning instruction on the assumption that in destroying American missiles just before they were launched, they would still save the lives of millions on the Soviet side.[18] Moreover, crucially, Tertrais and Pelopidas disagree about the importance of chance, the possibility of sheer bad luck, and about Tertrais's faith in human ability to prevent all – yes, all – dangerous misunderstandings that might arise from nuclear-related accidents, even when hypersonic missiles might be involved, which allow only seconds to make decisions. ... In international relations, one must always factor the possibility of unforeseen events into analyses – not as opportunity, however, but as a spoiler, a wild card, not as good fortune but as something that might derail all nicely laid out plans, signals and dispositions.[19] The problem is that, precisely as it is unforeseen at least in the time of its occurrence, one cannot factor in the way in which it will act as a spoiler; one can at best harbour a healthy or nerve-wrecking scepticism about anything ever going precisely according to plan.

Monocausal explanation fallacy

Taleb in two of his books attacks simplistic causal inferences from coincidences that may turn out to be random, occurring by chance, not by law or nature (or laws of the market).[20] This is also known as the 'false cause' bias, in which, *post hoc, ergo propter hoc*, something is seen as the outcome of something else merely because it can plausibly be explained as a consequence of the former and also occurred later. This leads us to the second methodological fallacy that is found particularly in the application of IR theories in IR departments. In most of them now, student essays, Master's dissertations and doctoral theses are constructed systematically on the social science pattern of expounding on one or more existing theory, then interrogating evidence to confirm or falsify the theory, and at

122 Knowns and Unknowns

best to refine it, but always sticking to the notion that there is such a theory that is either always applicable and explains everything, or that has to be discarded. Rolf Dobelli calls it 'the fallacy of the single cause'.[21] What is amusing is to see economists, and in some cases even natural scientists, shaking their heads in disbelief regarding such monocausal approaches. It should make any monocausally minded theorist think twice, that meteorologists, dealing with nothing but physics, are unable to predict the weather with any accuracy beyond ten days at best.

For Dobelli, this is linked to an atavistic search for a scapegoat and to conspiracy theories. We must admit that Thucydides made a famous contribution to this approach when he claimed, back in the fifth century BC, that the main driver of the Peloponnesian War was not an openly articulated reason: 'The truest cause I consider to be the one which was not talked about: the growth of the power of Athens, and the alarm which this inspired in Sparta, made war inevitable.' Yet even he thought it 'well to give the reasons spoken [grounds alleged] by either side, which led to the dissolution of the [previous peace treaty] and the breaking out of the war.' He then went into a detailed discussion of the relations between Corcyra and Epidamnus and Athens and Sparta, disputes about trade and access to ports, opinions about these disputes among the elites of the cities, and so forth.[22] As with the outbreak of the First World War, where a series of crises before that of the summer of 1914 might have led to war but did not, this raises the question of the importance of triggers and of their timing.[23] The very fact that reality is complex and that it requires considerable concentration to follow the development of events in the run-up to war makes it oh-so-much easier to seize upon a bigger 'cause' that seems to explain all. Few readers thus remember the intricacies of the quarrels of Corcyra and Epidamnus; most just remember the supposedly 'truest cause'. What makes this particularly memorable for those prone to believing in

Knowns and Unknowns

123

conspiracies is that Thucydides presented this 'truest cause' as the underlying, secret, unarticulated one.

Nevertheless, when we analyse international relations, a state government's (usually collective) behaviour (see above on the fallacy of monolithic governments) and other governments' responses, we must allow for the multiplicity of factors that influence these. There are the hard material factors that Marx emphasized; there is the interest of those in power to secure their positions; there are values that are invoked and that rally support for a cause (or fail to do so when the resentment of sacrifice outweighs the ethical drive); and there is chance. Chance is a major factor that no amount of planning can entirely eliminate – however much the strategic thinkers of the Enlightenment tried to by focusing on lines of operations and supplies and subjecting them to geometric formulae.[24] It is the minor detail – sometimes referred to as Cleopatra's nose (that charmed both Caesar and Mark Antony) that can, in captivating the attention of strategists, change their plans and ultimately lead them to ruin. Clausewitz famously recognized that chance continued to play a huge role. Instead of trying to eliminate it, he urged his posthumous readers to factor it into their analysis.[25] Moreover, both he and, before him, Napoleon thought that an ingenious commander could seize an unforeseen development as an opportunity that might be exploited in his favour.[26]

The attempts of partisans of this or that IR theory to explain the world in terms of their own theory alone creates systematic blinkers to the realization that, even in one-party dictatorships, there is competition near the top and there are differences of opinion. The problem with theories concerning human relations is that their creators aspire to see them as generalizable and universally applicable. Thus, whenever there is evidence of the theory not working in reality, many theoreticians of IR try to tweak the theory so as to make it applicable to every recorded instance (or they disregard the instance for some reason). To be fair, there are others who acknowledge that 'no International Relations theory has all the answers when it comes to explaining world politics in a global era',[27] but I have yet to see that insight echoed in IR students' essays.

Russian military authors writing on strategy in particular are also guilty of such monocausal approaches. A classic example is this: the government of F. D. Roosevelt in the Second World War supported resistance movements against the Germans and Japanese. American governments continued this policy in the Cold War, this time against communism, an essential part of their rollback strategy. (When it came to the crunch in 1954 and 1956, however, and there were uprisings in East Germany and Poland and later in Hungary, the Americans did not make good on their promise to such movements to come and support them materially, so the support was half-hearted.) From this, the Russians deduced that *all* resistance movements must be funded by America. Taking it a step further (at any rate, for propaganda purposes, but the military literature seems to indicate that they believe it themselves), they assume that all resistance movements and insurgencies against governments are not only *funded* by the CIA but would not exist without the machinations of the CIA. This of course hugely underestimates the discontentment and the ability to organize themselves among many dissidents the world over.

As I have already suggested above, instead of applying Procrustean theories, it is more helpful to look for *patterns*, as a pattern need not apply all the time, or even 50 per cent of the time, but can still be a useful analytical tool.

The Great Conditioning Ideal (Myth) and its sudden collapse

Even the savvier analysts who are sensitive to different mentalities and cultures may fall prey to faulty assumptions. Strategic cultures, or rather the collective mentalities of entire nations, are configured around clusters of beliefs, which may not be

Knowns and Unknowns   125

coherent but will be evoked time and again in the discourse about security and defence in the country concerned. They include, for example, the German tenet that 'war must never again emanate from our soil', or the French commitment to the defence of the 'sanctuary' constituted by the 'hexagon' of French national territory, or the Russian mantra that Russia has only two friends, its army and its navy.

But sometimes, such holy cows disappear with the smallest of puffs, unpredicted by the cultural specialist. In France, ever since the French Revolution, whenever France was a republic, there was the deep-seated belief that every (male) citizen should be willing to defend his country, and that this responsibility went hand in hand with his citizen rights. Thus universal (male) military service was part of the republican mindset. Similarly, the Federal Republic of Germany revived ideas connected with the resistance against French Occupation (itself indirectly inspired by the French Revolution!) to justify military service for its male youths. It turned out, however, in both cases that another variable was also at work: the perception of an external threat, actual or potential, that would necessitate such a large army and military training system. Seen by many commentators (including myself) as an unbudging part of the French and German republican collective mentality, it came as a surprise when in 1996 (to take effect in 2001) and in 2011 respectively, military service was suspended in France and Germany, practically without debate. It conformed to the ideals of both republics that it was suspended rather than abolished, as thus the idea of the citizen-soldier was not expunged entirely. Admittedly, the numbers of young men called up had already dwindled, leading to perceived injustice because of inequality among the generations concerned and, importantly, the need for large conscript armies was no longer perceived because, at the time, Putin seemed a guy one could get on with. Yet I for one had not seen this coming at all in the case of France, even though it made military sense (France's

126   Knowns and Unknowns

performance in the 1991 Gulf War had been hampered by not having large enough professional contingents to deploy, and draftees could not be sent out). Nor had I expected military service to be suspended in Germany without a huge debate.

More dramatic still was Sweden's abandonment of neutrality in reaction to Putin's all-out invasion of Ukraine in 2022. For Sweden, too, military service had been a national creed. During the Cold War, Sweden involved its entire society in a comprehensive territorial defence programme, with military service for all men in their youth and regular exercises for large proportions of men later in life. Here, too, national service was abandoned in 2008, during the inter-glacial period between the two Cold Wars, but in the Swedish case, it was more widely debated. Armed neutrality had been its political guideline since the Napoleonic Wars and in reaction to two previous centuries of Swedish imperial expansionism that had not ended so well when colliding with Russian and French imperial expansionism. Sweden, like Switzerland, had a self-perception of a peaceful but robust state that would fend off any invasion by itself, if ever it were to occur.

Swedish defence intellectuals had complained about this mantra of neutrality throughout the Cold War, and indeed its governments for some time went behind the backs of their population in coming to pragmatic albeit non-contractual defence arrangements with the United States in the 1950s and 1960s and again in the 2010s with the United States and NATO.[28] Also in 2017, given Russian behaviour, Sweden had reconstituted a more limited form of military service, now extended to include women, and Swedish staff officers began to turn up in NATO institutions and the staff colleges of NATO member-states. Over a few years, Swedish neutrality thus became increasingly hollow, even if it was still evoked by peace activists and women's associations. As Putin's Russia turned aggressive, the collapse in 2022 of Sweden's posture of non-alignment took place without serious opposition. Thus another holy cow expired, with very few protests, something external observers would have been hard-pushed to foresee ten years earlier. In short, those looking at strategic cultures must be aware not only of the *longue durée*, but they must also look out for signs announcing change, which can be profound.

Perhaps the greatest conditioning myth that has dominated western politics for decades of optimism after 1945 was that, given a free choice, the peoples of the world would espouse universal human rights, western-style democracy and capitalist economies. At least where human rights are concerned, this notion is rooted in the Age of Enlightenment, and, where the system of government is concerned, this was the positive idealism underlying such western colonialism as wanted to help the rest of the world turn itself into western-style democracies practising good governance. While the economic part is not entirely disproved, the idea that democratic constitutions are the *summum* of progress and would be preferred by all to unaccountable autocratic regimes has lost its power. Slowly but progressively, it did so in the 2000s and 2010s, with the western interventions in Iraq, various sub-Saharan African countries and Afghanistan. Arguably, it collapsed altogether with the western withdrawal from Afghanistan in 2021 and the lightning success of the Taliban in resuming power throughout the country. Think of the extraordinary ambition formulated by NATO back in October 2003, when it declared the 'end state' goal for its mission on behalf of the UN to lead an armed force into Afghanistan, namely, to create a 'self-sustaining, moderate and democratic Afghan government in line with the relevant United Nations Security Council resolutions, able to exercise its authority and to operate throughout Afghanistan, without the need for ISAF to help provide security'.[29] This ambition seemed crazy to anybody with even rudimentary knowledge of Afghanistan, an ethnically and socially extremely diverse state in which medieval elements predominated outside of Kabul. The belief, then, that

128 Knowns and Unknowns

human rights and democracy should be made available to and are deep down welcomed by all humans expired, again not with a bang but with a whimper, in 2021. It amounts to the de facto concession that the West is unable to help others *emerge from their self-imposed nonage* (to invoke Immanuel Kant). Instead, we have 'intervention fatigue' and the notion that there is little alternative to adapting to a world where the majority of states are ruled by autocrats, religious leaders or other forms of authoritarian dictatorships. The latter is reflected in the series of western national and alliance strategy concepts published since 2021.[30]

Box 3.1: Protest Movements and Binary Bias

There is something of a pattern when European powers or the US government supported protest movements in countries deemed to be unfriendly in the hope that the protesters would come to power and be friendlier. Underlying this is a reductionist binary view of the world: our enemy's critic must be our friend, and our critics must be in the pay of the enemy.

In the short term, German Chancellor Bethmann-Hollweg's decision in the First World War to let the communist exile Lenin travel through Germany and German-occupied territory to reach Russia where he contributed to the October Revolution had the desired effect: the revolutionaries not only overthrew the Russian government but under Lenin also pulled out of the war with a peace agreement greatly favouring Germany. In the long term, however, it led to the creation of the Soviet Union with its deep hostility not only to imperialist but also to democratic states on account of their 'capitalism'.

Similarly, in supporting the uprisings in Iran against the Shah, initially an amorphous but rather pro-democratic movement, President Jimmy Carter's administration hoped that the result would be a pro-western democratic state. Here, as in Russia in 1917 and after, a radical and well-organized faction

Knowns and Unknowns 129

seized the opportunity, in the case of Iran an Islamist faction, and the result was the Islamic State, infinitely more hostile to the West than the Shah had been.

There are parallels in the Arab Spring uprisings of 2010–12. Western countries harboured hopes that these would lead to the overthrow of authoritarian governments and their replacement by democratic state systems. Instead, Islamist factions, especially the Islamic Brotherhood, came to the fore in several countries, and we saw the rise of the 'Islamic State' and/or new autocratic regimes emerged. Generally – and this is a pattern, not a claim to universal applicability – protest is not enough, and protest movements are often hijacked by radical but well-organized groups, on whatever end of a political spectrum, from the Bolsheviks as in the Russian Revolution to Islamists in the other contexts cited. This should be a warning also to idealists everywhere: under a ruthless authoritarian leadership, democratic protests have little chance of succeeding. And if they do succeed, it tends to be the well-organized extremist leaders (communists, Islamists) who gain control in this way. The pattern can be traced back to the French Revolution.

The 'Colour Revolutions' in the early 2000s in successor states to the Soviet Union are an exception to the rule as they were not hijacked by extremist factions. Nevertheless, they met with fierce opposition from authoritarian regimes. In Ukraine, anti-democratic President Viktor Yanukovych, supported by Russian President Putin, attempted to reverse Ukraine's association with the European Union. But a democratic opposition, protesting in the *maidan*, the main square, prevailed, to the extreme annoyance of Putin in neighbouring Russia. A democratic Ukraine might always give bad ideas to opponents of his own ever more autocratic regime. Putin then misjudged his influence on this former Soviet Republic, and indeed the effectiveness of 'hybrid war' tools which he then employed from 2014 to force the protesters to give in so as to restore a pro-Russian government. When this strategy bore but little

130 Knowns and Unknowns

fruit, he launched the full-scale invasion of February 2022, his latest attempt to reverse Ukraine's westward drift.

Having learned their lesson, Putin and President Alexander Lukashenko of Belarus successfully forestalled a similar drift of Belarus into the democratic camp: the democratic opposition in Belarus now finds itself either in exile or in jail. The same applies to the opposition in Russia itself, of course – denigrated by Russian propaganda as agents of the West, many of its members held and hold quite critical views of the West. Either way, they are now muted, exiled, in jail or dead like Alexander Litvinenko, Sergei Magnitsky and Alexei Navalny.

* * *

The previous chapters have furnished ample evidence that psychologists' findings with regard to biases not only upset the neat assumptions of rational actor choices made in classical economics. They also apply to the realities in analysis and decision making in international relations. We can only trust our own judgements so far, and we can only expect an ally or an adversary (or another government department or company) up to a point to make decisions that derive entirely logically from *proclaimed* guiding principles of politics (as articulated, for example, in an election manifesto or a 'strategy' document).

It is thus a great challenge to know when to take official proclamations at their word. Should analysts have paid more attention to the vague but hatred-driven ruminations of Hitler's *Mein Kampf* than to his promises of peace in Munich in September 1938? Yes, without doubt, as the latter were quickly belied by his instructions to finish off Czechoslovakia in the following spring (see Box 0.1, p. 4). Should the professional analysts in the foreign embassies in Berlin have known which to trust more? Yes, in the light of the brutal repressive measures already taken in 1933–5 against Germany's minorities, whom Hitler and the National Socialist Party had declared enemies, and of Hitler's multiple breaches of the Versailles

Knowns and Unknowns

Peace Treaty's stipulations, including the rearmament of Germany. Might, in another place, another time, another radical party's leaders mellow when finally elected into government and confronted with the real tasks of ruling? Perhaps. There are examples of radical parties much reducing their goals when democratically elected into government as members of a coalition.[31] Here, as elsewhere, it is highly dangerous guesswork to project the experiences of one such party onto another. The dynamics of politics, and of governments, are complex, and how they play out depends on many players, structures and processes. That will be in part the subject of the next chapter.

4

Flaws and Quandaries of Strategy Making

Given all these biases that affect us and usually also our adversaries, it is not just foreign policy analysis but also policy and strategy making that are likely to be flawed, less than coherent, and may appear both irrational and illogical. Let us consider the implications.

A many-tentacled octopus?

We have already discussed the monolithic actor fallacy. Especially Russians, but probably also the leaders of other non-democracies, are particularly prone to the misperception that other states – including democratic states – and their alliances are monolithic actors driven by some shared inner logic. The penchant for conspiracy theories greatly reinforces this misperception. It was part of the 'operational code' (Nathan Leites and Alexander George), 'beliefs about political life', a *Weltanschauung*, the 'cognitive map' or the 'elite political culture' of Bolshevik analysts, and is still that of the Russian military literature of the post-communist era.[1] Even during the inter-glacial period of 1991–2007, Russian miltary writings

Flaws and Quandaries of Strategy Making   133

assumed consistently that across all the changing governments of the United States, Republican or Democrat, there had been a constant and enduring masterplan, using a huge array of different tools, from nuclear blackmail and arms races to Hollywood films and other instruments of soft power, to subvert and bring about the downfall of the Soviet Union. Little did Russian military experts of the 1980s or 1990s understand that the prevailing concept in the United States had become that of 'competitive strategy', associated with the influence that Andy Marshall had on the US government over several decades. This strategic approach started with the premise that the Soviet Union and the Warsaw Treaty Organization would continue to exist for the foreseeable future and that one had to adapt to long-term competition between the two systems, without an end in sight.

The systems of reward obtaining in democracies tend to encourage initiative in many areas, at least for more ambitious diplomats and military officers, and in smaller adjunct organizations such as cultural institutes or branches of the CIA. It is thus quite possible that, locally, agencies directly or indirectly acting in the interest of a democracy abroad come up with and then pursue initiatives they think are in line with their governments' aims. From the outside, the governments of major democracies, through the lens of 'monolithic actors', conspiracies and assumptions about coherent underlying masterplans, are thus seen as octopuses, with their many tentacles undulating in very different directions, yet – it is wrongly assumed – effectively controlled by a central brain.

Here is an example where the left tentacle of the US administration octopus did not know what the right tentacle was doing. In mid-1948, when the Yugoslav Communist Party was expelled from the Cominform (see Box 1.2, The Tito–Stalin Quarrel, p. 25), the British and American governments, on the advice of their embassies in Belgrade, had decided it was in their interests to help Tito stand up to Stalin. Unbeknown

134   Flaws and Quandaries of Strategy Making

to President Truman (who himself had approved this policy towards Tito) and to the State Department, however, the CIA seized the instability in Yugoslavia caused by this excommunication of the Yugoslav leadership to try to infiltrate Serb royalist exiles in Yugoslavia, just as they had only recently tried in Albania with Albanian exiles. Both operations were disasters. The Albanian operation was betrayed to Moscow by the British spy Kim Philby, while the landing of Serb royalists was betrayed to Tito by loyal compatriots. The American ambassador to Belgrade, Cavendish Cannon, only found out about the CIA's operation aiming to bring down Tito from the Yugoslav press when the infiltrated men were arrested. That operation of course sent confusing messages to Tito, obstructing his rapprochement with the West (Yugoslavia would remain resolutely 'non-aligned' thereafter).[2]

An example of the tail wagging the dog (or a tentacle of the octopus initiating a strategic approach) is that of how the United States became involved in supporting the Afghan Taliban in its resistance to Soviet occupation in the 1980s. This was famously initiated by a Congressman, Charlie Wilson, who as a member of the House Appropriations Committee was moved by members of the CIA to exploit a loophole in Congressional monitoring of defence expenses to finance the supply of arms to the Taliban. This story, carefully researched by the American journalist Charles Crile,[3] was popularized by the film *Charlie Wilson's War*, which fuses several actors into fewer roles for dramatic simplicity and in other ways has simplified the events. The events traced by Crile, however, turn around the CIA's historic Operation Cyclone, through which military supplies were purchased and delivered, and other forms of assistance initiated, not on the initiative, and initially also with little if any knowledge or oversight, of the main US administration.

Resulting attribution fallacy is especially common in the interpretations of such actions made by autocratic regimes, which, given the centralized authority of their own governments, assume that other governments and international organizations are monolithic actors with one central authority directing an overall masterplan from the top. They should know better as, even in autocratic regimes, there are silos of policy making and execution. Hitler's Third Reich deliberately worked on the principle of divide and rule, and Hitler bolstered his supreme authority by letting his subordinates and their respective organizations compete with one another. There were unintended consequences, as even he could not then be the supreme arbiter of all competing schemes presented. In anticipation of his imputed wishes, many a scheme was launched from within the various silos that was not directly initiated or closely supervised by Hitler, from Hess's aforementioned flight to Scotland to extend peace feelers to the detailed planning of the Holocaust.[4] Analogous examples exist for the Soviet Union and the East German state, where the secret service under Markus Wolf had considerable freedom of action.[5] It is sensible to presume that they could or can also be found in the policy making of the other states of the Warsaw Pact, for communist China or the Islamic Republic of Iran.

A classic example of the communist and post-communist Russian view of the United States as a gigantic octopus with its head as the White House and its tentacles everywhere acting out a masterplan is the Russian military leadership's reaction to an admittedly brilliant article written in 1992 by an American diplomat, Steven R. Mann. He was in the 1990s seen by Russian military authors as an *éminence grise*, whispering in the ear of the US president. Mann's area of expertise was the Central Asian republics (where he served as US ambassador in the mid-1990s) and energy resources around the Caspian Sea. From what we can tell, he did *not* run any clandestine agency pumping money into any democratic movements in the Central Asian states.[6] His article of 1992 spoke of inserting the 'virus' of 'democratic pluralism and respect for individual human rights'

136   Flaws and Quandaries of Strategy Making

into 'target populations', against the background of a major rethink of strategy that should get away from linear thinking centring on armed forces and tangible power.[7] For Russian observers, this revealed a secret global plan of the United States to weaken Russia further, post-Cold War, and Russian military literature elevated Steven Mann to the mastermind behind all American strategy since 1991.[8]

Another such figure presumed by Russian military authors to have designed a masterplan for destabilizing the Russian sphere of influence and, beyond that, the whole Arab world was Gene Sharp (1928–2018), a political scientist who taught mainly at the University of Massachusetts, Dartmouth, and had various connections with Harvard, and whose writings focused on non-violent means of resisting dictatorships.[9] For this, Sharp was repeatedly nominated for the Nobel Peace Prize. While his books and articles were clearly read widely, and may even have inspired individual leaders in 'Colour Revolutions', he can no more be depicted as the mastermind behind an American comprehensive strategy than Rousseau can be seen as the orchestrator of the French Revolution. And yet, with Steven Mann, Gene Sharp's name features repeatedly in Russian military writings as a key figure behind an American grand strategy aiming to break apart the Russian Federation and to loosen Moscow's grip on its friendly neighbours.[10] Andy Marshall's approach and influence, by contrast, seems to have gone largely unnoticed.

Similarly, the Iranian perception of Israel puzzles the outside observer. The mullahs' hatred of the 'Great Satan', America, has been extended to Israel as, supposedly, its obedient agent. The slightest knowledge of the rocky relationship between the United States and Israel belies this. On the American side, examples of disharmony range from Washington's scuppering of the Suez Operation in 1956 to trying to rein in Israeli war aims (successfully or unsuccessfully) in the various Arab–Israeli wars to pressure put on Israeli Prime Minister Benjamin

Flaws and Quandaries of Strategy Making 137

Netanyahu's regime in 2023 to abandon his plans for reforms of the judiciary. On the Israeli side, disobedience in all the above cases, and direct clashes such as the (deliberate) Israeli bombing of *USS Liberty* in 1967, or Netanyahu's blackmailing of President Clinton over the Monica Lewinsky affair in 1998 in return for a demand for stronger US support against the Palestinians – in this context revealing that Israel spies on the United States – all show that the Israeli government is anything but a tentacle of a big American octopus. But as dictatorships need enemies to keep their own populations down (with the excuse that this is necessary for national security), Israel, depicted as America's lackey, serves Iran as a useful – and nearer – proxy enemy, with secular Israelis and their lifestyles standing in for the 'moral depravity' of the West.

A final example of such dissonances in strategies can be found in China, if we can trust Edward Luttwak's analysis. There is, on the one hand, and for some decades already, the grand Chinese strategy of 'Peaceful Development' that goes back to Zheng Bijian, senior adviser to the government of Hu Jintao, general secretary of the Chinese Communist Party (CCP) from 2002 to 2012. Its essence is to increase China's influence through peaceful economic means while not upsetting any of China's neighbours – with whom China has countless border disputes – by sabre rattling. Yet China's armed forces are keen to increase their strength and their role. And, apparently, the Chinese Fisheries Administration's Law Enforcement Section that has its own navy of some five hundred ships is flexing its muscle and getting into fights with neighbouring countries such as the Philippines with which China has disputes about possessions in the South China Sea. These clashes, Luttwak argues, undermine China's peaceful expansion and defy the line theoretically imposed by the central government.[11] Without candid interviews or access to government archives, Luttwak's interpretation is difficult to verify, but the observation is difficult to dismiss that the respective strategies of a peaceful

138   Flaws and Quandaries of Strategy Making

rise to world power through trade and investment and of the intimidation of neighbours until they line up with your rival seem diametrically opposed to one another.

Bureaucratic politics

In all states, democratic or even autocratic (as no ruler can make do without his executive), bureaucratic politics – taken here to include the haggling, at government or any other level, between representatives of different parts of officialdom, be they government ministers, civil servants, officials or senior military commanders – obstructs the formulation of logically coherent policies and strategies. Bureaucratic politics, as analysts with experience of working inside US administrations have shown, is the bargaining and haggling among different actors within governments. They come to joint decision making each with their own agendas and preferences, often representing those of the parts of government – the ministry, department, agency, service – they represent. The bargaining process thus reflects policy goals way beyond those for which a particular strategy or policy is supposed to be crafted. Issues come into play (e.g., supporting the defence industry, or the lobby of Americans of Greek origin, in a senator's state) which have little to do with the original issue at hand (e.g., the overall structure of the defence budget, or relations with NATO-member Turkey).

Such differences are not new, at least not in European history. French Count Guibert, the leading strategic theorist in pre-revolutionary France, learned much about bureaucratic politics from his experiences of actual strategy making in the French war ministry. In 1770, he wrote,

> In almost all states of Europe, the different branches of administration are governed by particular ministers, whose interests and views jar, and are reciprocally detrimental to each other;

Flaws and Quandaries of Strategy Making 139

each of them is occupied exclusively with his object. One might imagine the other departments belonged to a different nation. Happy, indeed, are those States where the ministers, jealous of each other, do not act as open enemies.[12]

Forty years later, writing with the experience of Saxon and Prussian strategy making, Clausewitz's colleague Otto August Rühle von Lilienstern opined,

> [In] the History of the domestic affairs of any State, we see the war- and finance-ministers locked in eternal feuds, just as [with] diplomats and military commanders. . . . The war minister wants to increase the armed forces and asks one sacrifice after the other from the State; the finance minister tries to . . . keep expenses down . . ., so that he might produce a positive balance sheet . . . In short, each operates against the other, and eventually thus both harm the State.
>
> Why? Because the economic and the military constitution of the state must either be integrated fully, or else noxious differences will necessarily result from the self-centred efforts of each made without due concern for the other department (also acting in its own interest).

And he added:

> Unfortunately it is usually the case that . . . the supreme military commander is not given the necessary political explanations, and that . . . the main [foreign] policy maker has not taken the trouble to become acquainted with the simplest principles of the art of war. The government mechanism . . . usually keeps the two sectors well apart, especially in times of peace. If war breaks out, the necessary harmony is lacking everywhere. They make life difficult for one another, and it is lucky if the interests of the State are not buried by the hostile wrangling between diplomacy and the art of war.[13]

140   Flaws and Quandaries of Strategy Making

Today, with an all-of-government approach to writing 'national security strategies', there are far more government departments involved in the wrangling over the outcome than merely foreign and defence ministries, as we shall see presently. Thus now more than ever, strategies and policies are subject to the influence of diverging interests of different government departments. The aim of finding compromises within governments and alliances may well outweigh the aim of crafting an effective and coherent strategy to deal with the issue at hand.

Decision-making cycles

Further reasons why governments and indeed alliances are not coherent actors is that decisions have to be made about issues that occupy different time spans. The comprehensive 'national security strategies' that are composed under many different headings need to cover many of these. There may be the need to react quickly to a crisis, as with the documents that were produced or quickly 'refreshed' around the time of the Russian all-out invasion of Ukraine in February 2022. There are the cycles of governmental elections which in democracies are usually around four to five years. Autocratic regimes in which leaders can make themselves dictators for life have a much easier job there: they can usually both dictate to their industries and define targets tens of years ahead. Thus Xi Jinping in October 2021 promulgated the 'Resolution of the CCP Central Committee on the Major Achievements and Historical Experience of the Party over the Past Century', setting strategic targets to be reached by 2049, such as military parity with the United States and the integration of Taiwan into the People's Republic of China.[14]

In all types of government, there are decisions of defence procurements which, depending on the weapons or system, can take, say, two or three years for the acquisition of off-the-shelf products (when the time is merely spent on negotiating

Flaws and Quandaries of Strategy Making 141

the treaties and perhaps adding a few extras) to ten or more years for the construction of ships, which then may be in service for forty years, sometimes longer – the consequences of such a procurement decision can thus commit successive governments of different political hues. My favourite story in this context is that of the Royal Danish Forestry Commission which was given orders, after the British sinking of the Danish fleet in harbour in Copenhagen in 1807, to grow the oak trees for a new fleet. They reported back in 2007, task accomplished, the oaks were fully grown . . .

Other expenses need to be factored into strategic defence budgeting. Pensions for service personnel engaged at the age of twenty today will still imply costs to governments sixty-plus years on. Energy supplies of the future against the background of attempts to mitigate climate change have to be factored in, ensured through extensive development of 'green' sources of energy, to take effect over far, far longer stretches of time (and concomitantly with nefarious effects, if such 'green' sources are not developed). And currently considerations of how to store the wastage of the production of nuclear weapons and the generation of nuclear energy take the cookie, where safe storage over thousands and tens of thousands of years may be necessary. Yet all these things have to be budgeted for simultaneously.

The larger governments are, the longer it takes for a strategic decision to be made at the top and then to percolate down into concepts and policy papers flowing from this. So, in theory, there are strategic concepts that are put together at state or even alliance level. This usually takes a year or longer to draw up in endless committee meetings with representatives of many departments of governments or ministries or all the services. In turn, they are supposed to be the capstone documents from which regional or thematic sub-strategies or military planning documents flow. These can, however, take so long to formulate in collective decision making, again usually involving different

142   Flaws and Quandaries of Strategy Making

parties, that the capstone document is overtaken by events before its declination onto lower levels is complete.

This was notably the case with NATO's openly published Strategic Concept of November 1991 and the implementation, in a new (secret) Military Concept that was supposed to apply it to NATO's defence structures and capabilities. The Yugoslav Wars of Secession erupted that year and evolved over the following years to draw in NATO member-states, despite initial reluctance to get involved. The first Military Committee (MC) document MC 400 was adopted a month after the Strategic Concept, but soon needed updating. The Strategic Concept itself was not replaced until 1999, but in the meantime, MC 400/1 was issued in 1995, before both the Strategic Concept and a new document in the MC 400 series (MC 400/2) were updated in 1999.[15] A quarter of a century on, we have the same situation, where another document in the MC 400 series preceded the new NATO Strategic Concept of 2022, when in theory it should have been derived from it.

The MC 400/1 of 1995 in many ways departed from the political assumptions made at the higher Strategic Concept level; one was that the French government in this unpublished document proclaimed its willingness to cooperate with NATO structures in ways ruled out since France had left the integrated military structure of NATO back in 1966–7. In 1995, the French President Jacques Chirac favoured a return to the integrated military structure but, come 1997, he could not follow this through as, in a period of 'cohabitation', his prime minister Lionel Jospin headed another political party that opposed this. In Paris and even within NATO, French politicians, officials, officers and representatives were thus engaged in a subtle game in which one side used NATO's involvement in Bosnia-Herzegovina, the formulation of the 1995 document MC 400/1 and then of the Strategic Concept of 1999 and its application, MC 400/2, to bring France back into NATO's military structure, the other blocking this. In the end, France rejoined

Flaws and Quandaries of Strategy Making   143

only in 2009, when the configuration of NATO supporters in France's domestic politics was more favourable, in time for this to be reflected in NATO's new Strategic Concept of 2010.

This story not only illustrates that strategic concepts generally reflect a government's or an alliance's perceptions of the world *at the time* of issue, and the balance of interests within the government or alliance, and that they are mostly outdated as soon as they are published. It also shows that if they are published, they by definition pass over in silence or refer only obliquely to some politically sensitive matter. Finally, they illustrate the importance of decision-making cycles, a source of endless frustration for naive academics who would be policy advisers. For unless a government or alliance has been tasked to review its strategy or policies, and is in the initial fact-finding phase, there is generally no way of feeding in any new ideas. Effectively, there is only a short period in which, just after tasking, officials and military personnel are scrambling for ideas and might listen to experts – time permitting.

Sometimes, such brainstorming sessions with groups from many parts of government, other parts of the armed forces, business, even academia are factored into the early stages of crafting a new strategic concept. As the coordinator of a recent defence command paper (as defence strategies are called generically in the United Kingdom) estimated, around two thousand individuals must have been involved more or less in this process (mostly less). A recurrent bureaucratic fallacy can creep into such a process when it is strictly driven by the assumption that each 'ginger group' or 'workshop' meeting is supposed to produce a coherent text that *must* find its way into the final concept. This would, however, make the final text a shopping list. As Lord Ricketts, Britain's one-time national security adviser and coordinator of the United Kingdom's 2010 National Security Strategy, emphasizes, strategy making is about making hard choices, as no government has the means to do all it would like to do. Nor is it only a matter of limited

144   Flaws and Quandaries of Strategy Making

means, even for the United States or China, but also of mutually exclusive paths to follow. There are times when one must choose which horse to back in a race, or which side to ally with; playing several sides and not committing may make a government look duplicitous and untrustworthy, and it ends up being treated with suspicion by all sides.[16] The participation in the brainstorming phase can be extremely gratifying to outsiders and also gives the impression to different government sectors of 'having been consulted'. If they bother to read the final document, they will usually find, however, that the ideas, let alone formulations, they sought to bring in have not survived into its final form, at which point their enthusiasm for it will dwindle and may turn into outright criticism ('if only they had followed my advice . . .'). This, incidentally, explains the shortcomings of the monolithic actor fallacy discussed in chapter 1 above.

Later expert criticism coming after the publication of the document will usually only antagonize the practitioners and get the critics struck off the Christmas card list. All those involved in its drafting, especially in the final stages, will at that stage be convinced that no other choices and formulations were possible, given the priority of achieving consensus on the document – a task that, given the pressure of circumstances, normally ends up prevailing over any ambition to produce a work of inner coherence and cleverness, let alone wisdom, in approach. Nor will such critiques be of consequence, as chances are, given the rotation of personnel through different posts, that the next time such a document is written, it will be a different set of people who will be charged with the enterprise. And they will hardly start digging out the criticism made at the time of the previous publication.

Even with a much tighter timescale, decision-making cycles can be identified. When negotiations take place in a crisis context or shortly before summit meetings, there is of course the pressure to complete these, either as quickly as possible or

Flaws and Quandaries of Strategy Making 145

before a deadline (the summit, a deployment, the expiration of an ultimatum, . . .[17]). While an official's normal working day may be expected to end in the late afternoon, in these special contexts negotiations may well last into the evening. In my experience at NATO, there would then be pressure to come to a conclusion around 8 pm, when negotiators might still get to their offices to report back to capitals in the hope of getting instructions the following morning. Towards midnight, pressure would grow again as negotiators could still hope to get some sleep that night. Pressure used to fall off again after each of these timelines was reached. After midnight, one would assume that negotiations would automatically become 'all-nighters', so there was little point in keeping up the tempo; sometimes, breaks would then be made to report back to capitals before reassembling. Either way, at several times, as Sir David Omand put it, 'there will come a point in a prolonged debate in which the strong urge for the psychological relief of closure will come upon the group',[18] regardless of how much actual progress had been made.

A further, semi-independent decision-making cycle would underlie the whole process, that of Washington. Given the six-hour time difference between Brussels and Washington, and the American policy-making process which, as we have noted, tends to leave little leeway for negotiations for US negotiators, all of NATO's activities tended to begin later and end much later (if you were among those officials concerned with crises or ministerial meetings and communiqués) than those of other government ministries or public services. NATO meetings thus tended to start late and, often enough, would break up as the American representatives waited for instructions from Washington. Kahneman and Dobelli cite research showing that judges are more severe or lenient in the penalties they deal out, depending on the time of day (and distance from meals)[19]; similar observations can be made about the work of committees on strategy making.

146   Flaws and Quandaries of Strategy Making

Analogous pressures would then apply towards the end of the week. Some officials commuted to homes in other countries for the weekend, and we would be aware of whether this was the case for the presidents of particular committees and, in turn, have in mind the departure times of the last Eurostar for London, Paris or Amsterdam. One had a grudging admiration for those who did not show tenseness or heave a heavy sigh once the time passed when they could hope to catch that train, but that was no guarantee against their getting grumpier as the evening wore on. You can imagine that the pressure to come to an agreement increases further when a deadline looms, such as a ministerial meeting or the end of a big international conference where a result – usually in the form of a joint communiqué – is expected. In 1955, a conference in Messina (Sicily) to explore possible future reinforced European cooperation might well have failed to become that key step towards European integration for which 'the Messina Conference' is now famous.[20] No joint communiqué had been agreed upon by the time the social programme of the final evening was scheduled: a ballet in the Greco-Roman amphitheatre of Taormina, followed by a dinner in a former monastery turned into a luxury restaurant. Back in their hotel in Messina, the thoroughly inebriated delegates reluctantly let the Belgians under their determined leader Paul-Henri Spaak herd them into a hotel room, the latter insisting a communiqué had to be written there and then. Amazingly, the alcohol helped resolve some outstanding key differences between the leaders of the Belgian and French delegations (Spaak and Antoine Pinay respectively), and the result was a success.[21] (Since then, organizers of such conferences tend to be more prudent when planning for the last evening of a conference.)

Defence preparedness, at least on the NATO side, also underwent, and still undergoes, periodicities. Apart from a few times of extreme tension in the Cold War, barracks in many places emptied on the weekend. When the two Germanies

Flaws and Quandaries of Strategy Making 147

were united in 1991, East German military personnel who had been brought up to believe that NATO was prepared 24/7 for a surprise attack in the Warsaw Pact were astonished to find that their West German colleagues went home at midday on Fridays, not to return until Sunday evening or even Monday morning. This jarred with the picture which eastern propaganda had painted of the aggressive NATO, ever ready to pounce on the countries of the Warsaw Pact. In reality, the unpreparedness for war of Israel on Yom Kippur 1973 or even Sukkot 2023 would have been nothing compared with a Warsaw Pact weekend attack on the Central Front . . .

Holiday periods can also have nefarious impacts. The NATO countries' exit strategy from Afghanistan after the deployment of the NATO intervention force ISAF in 2003 had been planned for a long time and was initiated in 2014. Nevertheless, the timing of the last phase of American withdrawal in 2021 was chaotic when it was brought forward by President Joe Biden from the originally planned date of 11 September to August, despite an observed surge in Taliban operations and the geographic extension of their control. July and the first half of August being the traditional European summer holiday period, the British and German governments that still had troops in Afghanistan were caught by surprise. Unable to keep their own forces in place once the Americans pulled out, their own withdrawal was shambolic. Worse still, their good intentions of bringing out Afghan interpreters and other support staff who were unlikely to thrive under vindictive Taliban rule were poorly implemented in practice, with enormous consequences for many individuals and their families.[22]

Systems of incentives condition the behaviour of organizations

Rolf Dobelli in his insightful study of human biases claims that 90 per cent of an organization's behaviour is conditioned by incentives.[23] While such a figure seems to underestimate what

148   Flaws and Quandaries of Strategy Making

people would do for their ideals, even this is bound up with incentives. We have already discussed the mindset leading Christian Crusaders to risk their family fortune for campaigns from which they might not return in the firm belief that this would give them absolution from the sins. Christians fighting those of other Christian denominations in the confessional wars of the fifteenth to eighteenth centuries would also be fighting for the salvation of their souls. Nationalists and socialists in the wars and uprisings of the nineteenth and twentieth centuries fought for a common cause which might leave them dead but honoured as heroes of the nation or the revolution. Jihadi suicide bombers seem motivated by the prospect of Paradise with its dubious reward of encountering a batch of giggling and squealing pubescent girls, but perhaps also, more seriously, by material rewards promised to their families by the Jihadist organization. (This hope for reward was expressly targeted by the Israeli Defence Forces when destroying the family homes of suicide bombers.) The British system has its knighthoods and many-tiered honours lists, the French its *Légion d'honneur*, the German its *Bundesverdienstkreuz*, none of which cost the taxpayer much more than the award ceremony.

In less adrenaline-driven bureaucratic processes, especially in times of peace, there may still be a fusion of the belief that one is fighting for a noble cause that will be judged worthy by history, and of personal promotion which one can explain to oneself as being pursued in the interests of the cause. At any rate, the rapid deployment cycles of military officers, and only slightly less so of diplomats, put great pressure on them to be *seen* to make a difference, at least by their superiors who will evaluate their performance. Future positions are assigned on the basis of evaluations, of course. As a consequence, it is an unattractive proposition to continue longer-term schemes initiated by predecessors, while a new position calls for new proposals, new initiatives, new policies. On the upside, this may mean that policies are tried anew (under different labels)

Flaws and Quandaries of Strategy Making 149

which, due to adverse circumstances, had failed in the past and which the previous incumbent of that post did not have the courage to revive when perhaps they should have. A little later, the time may be ripe for a breakthrough.

On the downside, applying long-term policies that can only bear fruit over time is an unattractive proposition as it yields no recognition in the short term, and many a good policy may thus be discarded prematurely. The French education system is a particularly famous example for such constant tampering and change, as are foreign aid schemes, but also, important for our purposes, *operations extérieures*, foreign interventions. Think of Indochina/Vietnam by France and then the United States from the late 1940s until the early 1970s, Afghanistan by the USSR in the 1980s and then the US-led coalition of 2001–2021, and Iraq 2003–2011. Each new commander sent out attempted to implement change, going to considerable trouble to present the ideas and approaches on which it was based as new. Peruvian Admiral Luis Del Carpio calls this the 'Ctr+Alt+Delete Bias'. The picture painted by Michael Hastings in his book on the American military leadership in Afghanistan from 2001 illustrates the pattern even if its cinematic adaptation as *War Machine* (2017, dir. David Michôd) may exaggerate this somewhat.[24] But I must say that I became suspicious by the time I heard a third commander of British forces in Iraq telling an audience that there had been *no* proper strategy before *he* had arrived, and that *he* crafted one that now promised success.

Militaries still more than other bureaucracies require obedience and discipline. This stands in direct tension with the need to be open to change and to helpful ideas coming up from the bottom, or coming in sideways, going against a top-down approach of orders and implementation. This paradox is devilishly difficult to resolve. Many a clever officer's promotion and career is stunted because he or she thinks and argues too much; others are promoted because they say and do just what their superiors – and the government – like to hear and see.

150   Flaws and Quandaries of Strategy Making

An organization's system of rewards conditions its members' behaviour.

For those with initiative and ambition, however, crises and change may be seen as opportunities to promote a long-standing pet project (and themselves). Is not the election of a new president in Cerasia a chance for breaking a deadlock in debt-deferral negotiations? Is not the refugee crisis in Kamon the moment to obtain port access rights from Kamon's neighbour? Is not the putsch in Bothnia an opportunity to persuade Blueland to buy arms aid to fend off a possible invasion by the putschists? Is not the rescue of nationals from a port in Ruritania the opportunity to show off the new amphibious vessel and make the case for the purchase of more?

There are also examples of strategy making being influenced by the 'I wanna be there too' syndrome. Thus navies have in recent decades played a prominent part in military interventions in *landlocked* countries, and many officers from NATO countries will feel that their reputation in the services is linked to whether and, if yes, how many tours they did in Afghanistan, and that their careers will benefit or suffer accordingly.

Saying not doing

As in any walk of life, there are also great incentives for military officers and civil servants in all parts of government to claim achievements where there are few or none, and in any case to show evidence of having carried out orders and instructions. As a result, institutions will always try to present their activities in the best light. They can present activities of a minor sort as though they were very important and meaningful. One must pay careful attention and read between the lines to understand where little or no progress has been made.

Before NATO was created, indeed before the North Atlantic Treaty was signed in Washington in April 1949, five European countries had already signed a similar treaty of mutual

Flaws and Quandaries of Strategy Making 151

defence, which in fact included a much stronger commitment, not potentially subject to parliamentary veto as is the North Atlantic Treaty. This European treaty was signed a year earlier in Brussels, and created the Western Union, not the one to send money, but a defence pact initially specifically created against a potential resurgent German enemy. In the mid-1950s, it was renamed Western European Union, and by now the original signatories – the United Kingdom and France, which had initiated it jointly, plus the Benelux countries – felt sufficiently confident that no new Nazi Germany would rise out of the ashes of the old to include West Germany, and also Italy that had already been taken into NATO in 1949. When still five-partite, the Western Union had created a small defence organization, but delegated most of its defence cooperation and infrastructure building and so on to NATO. The Western European Union Organization continued to exist until 2007, when the commitment to mutual defence it entailed was absorbed into the European Union's basic constitution, signed off at Lisbon that year. Seen from the outside, it was difficult to tell that it merely had a shadow existence: it had regular defence ministers' meetings where communiqués were produced, officers and diplomats were assigned to its headquarters, and some sort of business was conducted there, if only to file regular reports on the troop strengths of member-states. The British Defence Secretary Denis Healey called it no more than a 'dining club'. But if you went strictly by the existence of organizations and their structures, by regular statements and other signs of activity, there was a European defence agency, all these years, alongside NATO. (Now that we might need it, however, it no longer exists.)

This is merely an example to illustrate how difficult it is, if one is merely doing a systematic survey of existing organizations or government agencies and so on, to find out which parts actually matter and are important, and which ones are not. Similarly, for somebody studying the who is who and

152   Flaws and Quandaries of Strategy Making

what part of government matters in, say, Myanmar or China, or even Turkey, it is not immediately obvious where the real work is done, where the real power lies, the real influence. In democracies and even in dictatorships, this may change over time, as new sections are created and old sections are very rarely closed down. In the German Ministry of Defence, there was until 2023 a section called 'Military Strategy', but its only subsection that also had 'Strategy' in its title dealt exclusively with intelligence.

Box 4.1: Teasing Your Ally: De Gaulle's Flirtation with the USSR, 1966–7

There can also be entertaining sides to this. André Finkelstein, who was deputy director general of the International Atomic Energy Authority from 1969 to 1973, and before and after that, a high-ranking official in the French Atomic Energy Commission, in an oral history session shared an example of this. It concerns a visit to the French nuclear research facility at Pierrelatte by a group of Soviet nuclear scientists, following the Franco-Soviet Declaration of 30 June 1966 that announced various forms of technological collaboration.[25] This was against the background of de Gaulle's rather prickly relationship with the United States, and his bid to restore France to great power status by distancing himself from the United States (and from NATO – he pulled France out of the integrated military command that year) and flirting with the Soviet Union, making sure both treated France with respect. The scientists' visit was made very public, and the brouhaha in the American press was to be expected. What actually happened, according to Finkelstein, was that the Soviet scientists were brought into the entrance hall of Pierrelatte, and a series of long and cordial speeches about the friendship between the peoples of the world ensued, slowly translated each time, sentence after sentence, from Russian into French and French into Russian. Then

Flaws and Quandaries of Strategy Making 153

the entire party together with their French hosts – neither of whom spoke the other's language – was carted by bus to Les Baux de Provence, a site of stunning beauty and of a three-star Michelin restaurant, where cordiality increased when the company was wined and dined appropriately. At around three in the afternoon, the Soviet visitors were given the difficult choice of either returning to Pierrelatte for further laboriously translated exchanges or finishing up with an old Cognac and a good cigar. After not all too extensive deliberation, the Soviet physicists chose the latter.[26]

Since the 1960s, France and (West) Germany have gone to considerable lengths to bury the past – centuries of sibling rivalry going back to Charlemagne's empire being broken up into independent rivalling entities that would eventually become France and Germany. This led to annual summits between French presidents and (West) German chancellors, at times joined by their ministers. Here, subjects of particular concern to one or the other side tended to be aired, and joint statements would draw up agendas of subjects subsequently to be discussed at working level by government ministries concerned with these.

In the 1980s and 1990s, one such matter of concern to the Federal Republic of Germany (including after reunification) was France's short-range ground-to-ground nuclear missiles, and how France might use these in a war against oncoming Warsaw Pact forces: German defence experts feared that they might be used from French soil to wipe out a wave of Soviet and other Eastern tanks as they were rolling across West Germany towards the French border. In other words, they would detonate on West German territory. Even if they were to be moved forward into German territory – a technical possibility as they were mobile – chances were they would be used on targets in Germany. In 1988, a Franco-German Defence Council was created with much fanfare, which the German Chancellor Helmut

154   Flaws and Quandaries of Strategy Making

Kohl and his government hoped would be the forum for discussing France's short-range nuclear weapons – perhaps to the point of it becoming a sort of bilateral Nuclear Planning Group like that in NATO of which France was not a part. Repeatedly, communiqués issued by this Council expressed the intention of addressing this subject. The very repetition indicated, however, that such meetings never materialized. Eventually, these French short-range missiles were withdrawn altogether. The point, from an analytical perspective, is that it would have been unclear to a superficial observer what this Council was achieving and what importance it had.[27]

In short, in government, much more is said than done, much more announced than carried through. It is not enough to amass evidence of statements of good or grand intentions as evidence of correlated actions. Many an announcement of a tidal turn overstates what really happens, and time and again commentators fall for it. Thus announcing great extra spending on defence may merely mean, in practice, that projects previously agreed but put on ice are finally unfrozen, and that money previously assigned to these projects is finally spent. Indeed, the defence procurement books of a state may well be cooked, hiding actual spending figures even from allies.[28] As officers and officials have every reason to present what they are doing in the best possible terms, there need not be a conscious intention to deceive, to mask reality with exaggerations of success and great performance. Consequently, seeing through that glitter of presentation for an analyst of an accountable democracy may be different in degree, not in substance, to what it is to try to interpret what an autocratic regime is doing.

The 'not-invented-here syndrome'

Closely connected with performance incentives and punishments is the 'not-invented-here syndrome'. Officials and officers are protective of their own areas of competence, the areas assigned to them by administrations. Bureaucracies – especially old, established bureaucracies – define the criteria for positions and salaries at different levels within a hierarchy by the number and importance of subjects covered, and by the number of subordinates an administrator has. Every civil servant, every military officer, every bureaucrat knows that any shift in the importance of subjects, any move of responsibility for a specific file from one policy officer to another, any appointment of more personnel here which might lead to the reduction of personnel there might be detrimental to their own position and pay grade. Moreover, it is likely to benefit a competitor in the race for promotion to a more limited number of posts at a higher level of the hierarchy. Then there is the implicit question, if this initiative concerns your *chasse gardée*, why it was somebody else who came up with this idea and not you. Thus incentives to support a competitor's scheme are automatically overshadowed by such considerations.

This applies even to recommendations coming from outside. They may be brilliant, and the official to whom they are put may realize that they would fit beautifully into the current trend of thinking and provide the solution to a problem of its implementation. But many an official has been exposed to ideas flowing out of academia that simply misunderstand the constraints and obstacles of bureaucratic policy making: the limits on budgets given to individual sections of departments, the effort it would cost to persuade superiors to run with this project and to campaign for the redistribution of funds or the appropriation of special slush funds for this project, the jealousy this would evoke among colleagues, and so on. Many a bureaucrat, especially later in life, having experienced their share of frustrations, will heave a heavy sigh, mutter something about an ideal world and shelve the proposal.

156   Flaws and Quandaries of Strategy Making

Mixed signals: Destroying, preserving or mediating?

There is also a profound difference in the cultural approaches
to conflicts and crises of different parts of a government
machinery. The raison d'être of any military is the assumption of a hostile environment, of the existence of antagonists
and indeed committed enemies, and they should plan for the
worst, even if that is unlikely to arrive. Yes, militaries can be
good at organizing things in crisis contexts, they can be good at
taking on policing functions, they can be asked to deliver food
aid and send their sappers to repair bridges, and they may play
a key role in keeping order and guarding against breakdown in
a peace-building context. Their forte, however, is or should be
warfare in its many variations. Everything else is an accessory.
Accordingly, their basic view of the world is conflictual, their
assumption is that the environment is hostile, that even non-
violent contexts are precarious. 'Others', natives in crisis areas,
are seen as potential 'hostiles' against whom one has to be on
one's guard; indeed, oneself and one's fellow soldiers' lives may
depend on doing so. If necessary, their mission is to kill and
destroy.

This approach is diametrically opposed to that of the
Red Cross or aid agencies, or also government departments
charged with administering aid to developing countries or
crisis areas. These see the civilians – and wounded soldiers, in
the case of the Red Cross! – as potential victims of violence, to
be protected, nursed and sheltered. They see the environment
as something that must also be protected; it consists of the
shelters, the food, the livelihood of those whom these agencies
are there to help. The immediate need of militaries to destroy
in order to protect themselves will conflict with the desire of
governmental development agencies to assure the long-term
well-being of civilians and civilian society in conflict areas.
The quarrels between the British Department for International
Development and the Ministry of Defence which took place

Flaws and Quandaries of Strategy Making 157

between 1997 and 2020 were proverbial, as were those between the ministers representing these respective ministries. Again, no wonder that government policies are perceived as puzzling abroad when their different parts have clearly divergent priorities.

Diplomacy is based on the fundamental assumption that there are mutual interests in collaboration or, in the case of conflicting interests, that there is scope for negotiation, mediation and compromise. Diplomats are conditioned to look for non-violent solutions to conflicts, to leave doors open for a new rapprochement, for a peaceful solution short of fighting, or in the case of outright fighting, for making peace. Leaving doors open, indeed the penchant for never closing them,[29] a bias found not only in government, can prevent the coherent pursuit of a deterrent or even a coercive strategy, leading to appeasement instead.

Box 4.2: The Falklands War, 1982

The Falklands, aka the Malvinas, are a group of islands, disputed between Argentina and the United Kingdom, off the east coast of Argentina. Successively, they have been claimed by a number of countries. They have been under British control since 1833, but Argentine governments have long argued that the British illegally seized the islands that should have come to Argentina when it became independent of the previous owner, Spain, back in 1819. Diplomatic negotiations about their status have taken place on and off since 1968, with the UN urging negotiations given to resolving the issue (implying a recognition of some question over the islands' ownership). In 1977, a naval incident involving a British and an Argentine ship was played down by the British government. At the time, there was concern that the Argentinian junta that had seized power in 1976 might invade the islands, and the British government despatched two Royal Navy frigates and a submarine to the

158   Flaws and Quandaries of Strategy Making

Southern Atlantic. Plans for an invasion were temporarily shelved in Buenos Aires.[30]

Pressure to reach a settlement once again intensified in 1980 when the military junta on the one hand sought results, and a British junior minister's willingness to compromise with a leaseback scheme was blocked by a jingoistic House of Commons. At the end of 1981, the Argentinian junta under General Leopoldo Galtieri, Air Brigadier Basilio Lami Dozo and Admiral Jorge Anaya decided to revive invasion plans, setting a date for mid-1982. The date was brought forward to 2 April 1982 after an incident on 19 March involving Argentinian citizens who raised an Argentinian flag on one of the islands, to which Prime Minister Margaret Thatcher responded by merely sending out an ice patrol vessel from the main harbour of the islands, Port Stanley.[31] A subsequent inquiry, known as the Falkland Islands Review (also known as the Franks Report after its chairman), concluded that the British government's low-key responses, the continuing arms sales to Argentina and the refusal to grant the Falkland Islanders full British citizenship 'may have served to cast doubt on British commitment to the Islands and their defence'.[32]

It was only after the actual invasion started and was confirmed that the Thatcher government reacted unambiguously, sending naval and ground forces from European waters to the South Atlantic. Britain had the backing of a UN Security Council resolution calling for the withdrawal of Argentinian forces, negotiated between 1 April, when Britain received reports of the imminence of the invasion, and 3 April. The ensuing war lasted until 14 June 1982, with casualty figures (British and Argentinian) totalling less than 1,000. It resulted in the fall of the Argentinian junta, but left the islands an unresolved problem in British–Argentinian relations.

Flaws and Quandaries of Strategy Making 159

The Falklands War of 1982 resulted in part from the reluctance, first, of the British government to assume firm deterrent postures (such as to send armed forces to the South Atlantic in full view of the world, rather than secretly despatching a submarine in 1977) and, then, by the Buenos Aires junta's miscalculation that this signalled weakness. When the Argentinian invasion occurred, London reacted more strongly to this breach of international law than a narrow cost–benefit calculation regarding the retention of the islands themselves would have suggested – indeed, the British Foreign and Commonwealth Office in particular had already shown a willingness to negotiate *peacefully* about a cession of the islands to Argentina, negotiations it did not want to see undermined by strong military postures. The result was war, resulting from mutual misunderstandings.

The reluctance to close doors can seize hold of entire governments, and we have seen it go strong in the West in attitudes towards Russia, after the Russia–Georgia War, even after Russia's oblique intervention in Ukraine from 2014, and in Europe's and many other countries' approaches to China. Unwillingness to close doors to compromise and to peaceful outcomes, that is, to foreclose alternative policy options, is to the credit of democracies and a sign of their fundamentally pacific intentions. Nevertheless, it often results in incoherence in the overall strategy or policy, and in any case signals confusingly contradictory approaches.

How to know what's best

What is the smaller evil in the long run?

European civilizations and their issues are conditioned to see the world in moral binaries, good and evil, friend and foe. While every age must have produced its pragmatists, it was a Christian bishop living around 400, Augustine of Hippo,

160 Flaws and Quandaries of Strategy Making

who recognized and advised on the fact that many decisions – especially in contexts of war and peace – are choices not between good and evil, but between two evils. His advice was to choose the lesser, of course, while not deluding oneself that it is a wholly *good* option. War is always an evil, but so may be standing aside while innocents are slaughtered somewhere. Once the choice between two evils is recognized, the problem becomes how to judge which is the lesser of the two.

This is where another bias needs mentioning that in itself is a very good thing: compassion. Unfortunately, as Daniel Kahneman has noted, we as human beings have great difficulties relating to statistics, while we can feel compassion for individual cases. Stalin is often quoted with the dictum that 'a single death is a tragedy, a million deaths are a statistic', and he certainly behaved accordingly. Seized by compassion for a few compatriots taken hostage in Lebanon and for their families, under pressure from the media, US President Ronald Reagan became emotionally obsessed with the task of freeing them (after all, what is a president if he cannot even protect or rescue his own countrymen?). He was drawn into the Iran–Contra affair, in which he authorized the supply of arms to Iran in the hope of persuading Iran's theocratic government to order their clients Hezbollah, the hostage takers, to free the hostages, with little or no result but relatively worse second- and third-order consequences.[33] Israel's governments have also repeatedly been pressured by public opinion to go to great lengths to free Israeli hostages taken by Palestinian terrorist groups, such as the soldier Gilad Shalit who was held from 2006 to 2011 and the 250 hostages taken by Hamas in 2023.

Assuming that we are even capable of thinking rationally about what would be the smaller evil, in the sense of leading to the suffering of *fewer* people (and not just our own people), how can one know in advance which option would have what result? What will be the first-, second- and third-order consequences of any option, intended and, above all, unintended?

Flaws and Quandaries of Strategy Making 161

This question leads us directly to our collective inability to foretell the future. While individual experts and a few governments courageously sketch likely future developments, professional forecasters keep emphasizing their inability to *predict* the future with any confidence, let alone precision. There are certain long-term trends, yes, but even those could in future accelerate, increase or slow down, decrease, or do something in the middle, and then there are the unknown unknowns discussed above, the wild cards or black swans which can take us by surprise, yet decisively change the trajectories of some trends and put an end to others. This is why futurologists now all try to devise exercises for flexible adaptation to unforeseen developments while modestly admitting that one cannot predict the future in human relations given their complexity.

Accordingly, it is supremely difficult to judge, in advance, what the consequences of a state's action in matters of war and peace will be. The futurologist running the Delphic Oracle enterprise who was consulted by Lydian King Croesus when he considered crossing the River Halys to fight the Persians in the sixth century BC apparently faced the same difficulty and chose to keep her formulation nicely ambiguous: she merely said that if he did so, he would destroy a great empire, not whose that would be. As he misread the pronouncement as a go-ahead, the campaign's outcome was bad for Croesus.

One great quandary in a critical situation that could tip into war is whether a government admits what it knows from its intelligence sources. A range of difficult factors come into play here. Should one 'burn' one's intelligence source, which may actually mean sacrificing to the enemy's wrath loyal human beings who have risked their lives for one's side? Should one risk losing this source – which may just be a particular way of culling signals intelligence which the enemy thus discovers – so that it is likely to be blocked in future? But then there is also the question as to when an enemy leader decides to go to war.

162   Flaws and Quandaries of Strategy Making

He or she may have created the option of doing so, but may also still be willing to call it off. How is such a tense situation affected by one's own actions? It is said that in some NATO member-states, governments issued a blanket interdiction of any contingency planning for a Russian invasion of Ukraine until mid-February 2022, when in rapid succession Emmanuel Macron and Olaf Scholz travelled to Moscow (separately, of course) in the fond hope of warding off that decision. Both leaders were afraid they would push Putin into action, rather than pull him away from the brink if they went *after* having drawn up plans on how to support Ukraine against Russia.

Indeed, the impressively poor performance of Russian forces at the beginning of this 'special military operation' has led to speculations that leading Russian officers up to the highest levels were kept in the dark about Putin's plans, and still believed just before the invasion was given the go-ahead that the entire deployment of Russian forces was indeed an 'exercise'. *Was* there still room for negotiations and mediation in mid-February 2022? Would these have diminished if contingency plans for the support of Ukraine had been drawn up prior to this? Would they perhaps even have been more successful if such plans had existed and had become known in the Kremlin? Which way might the situation have tipped?

'Sunk cost fallacies' and windows of opportunity

This problem of anticipating outcomes not only obtains when decisions are made as to whether to go to war or not. They also weigh heavily when the going gets rough and one begins to wonder at what point one should cut one's losses. This can be where a 'sunk cost fallacy' comes in, which we know from gambling contexts. In the military context, it is the often self-delusory notion that past sacrifices can be given meaning by making more sacrifices in the hope of turning one's luck. This is reminiscent of the gambler who has incurred great losses but

Flaws and Quandaries of Strategy Making   163

borrows money in the hope of recovering them. Consequently, there are lists of military interventions which dragged on but were ultimately unsuccessful, from France's involvement in Indochina and Algeria, the American war in Vietnam and the USSR's intervention in Afghanistan, followed by that of NATO forces a good decade later. This particular bias overlaps with 'loss aversion bias', also known as 'prospect theory': nations tend to fight harder to prevent the loss of territory held at the outset of a war than to win new territory.

Last but not least, there is the danger of being persuaded to go to war thinking this is the last opportunity of doing so before a dangerous adversary becomes too strong to be checked. We have already referred to Thucydides' view that the 'truest' but unavowed cause of Sparta's unleashing war against Athens in the fifth century BC was the fear of Athens' growing influence. Similar 'last chance' or 'window of opportunity' thinking can be found a number of times in European history. One permutation is that which the historian Stig Förster diagnosed for the bad decisions leading to the First World War.[34] The German expression 'fleeing ahead', towards the enemy, towards danger, in the hope of catching the other side by surprise or by sheer bravado, also describes this particular catastrophic episode of European history. We have already noted the miscalculation that can arise when somebody cries 'wolf' more than once. Here we encounter a variant, which is to think one can benefit from a crisis, the $n + 1$st crisis, in the confidence that it will not degenerate into war – because one has got away with it on previous n occasions (see the example of the trusting poultry above).

On satisficing and bounded rationality

All of the above will hopefully have raised questions about the rationality not only of intelligence analysts and strategy makers, but also of all of us. Lawrence Freedman has summed

164   Flaws and Quandaries of Strategy Making

up the challenge posed by psychologists and neuroscientists to economists very helpfully. The former have furnished plentiful evidence that people are 'subject to mental quirks, ignorance, insensitivity, internal contradictions, incompetence, errors in judgment, [and] overactive or blinkered imagination'.[35]

Normal humans might still approximate *Homo economicus*, the supposed rational actor presumed by the economist, in their behaviour if they behave *relatively* reasonably. They might not compare the prices of espresso machines in every shop in town, as according to economists they should. In real life, nobody would have the time to do this. They may, however, compare enough to make a reasonable decision of where to buy theirs. This would not satisfy the criteria for being a perfect *Homo economicus*, but it might – here the neologism invented for this purpose – *satisfice* the requirements of the situation. Equally, and more importantly for our subject, decision makers act on the beliefs and information they have (see section 'Too little or too much knowledge', p. 108), and on their own wishes (which includes their wishful-thinking interpretations of a situation). In sum, they act within their 'bounded rationalities' (Alexander George), another term we owe to this controversy.

For many situations in life, satisficing and acting within bounded rationalities may be sufficient, even in international relations, where decisions may affect the lives of very many people. It will never make decisions conform entirely to the standards of rational actor theory, however.

* * *

The more one contemplates the workings of governments, the more one is reminded of the old image of a storm-tossed ship in largely uncharted waters, unable to take its bearings from sun or stars under a cloudy sky, with unending disputes about what to do first, whether to aim for a distant coast where Cyclops might lurk or to sail on, which of the monsters arising from

Flaws and Quandaries of Strategy Making

the deep to fight first while keeping the crew in line and the hungry passengers from staging an uprising as fresh water and victuals are forever in short supply. It is probably the brutal, ideology-driven regimes, those that don't mind throwing some unruly passengers overboard while others are starving, and letting a few sailors walk the plank, who can most coherently and single-mindedly steer their ships full-speed ahead – but this may mean onto the next reef or the next iceberg. They tend to have a longer time in government than do democratic regimes which enables them to stay on their extremist course, following the siren song of their particular ideology that promises a perfect world. There is some solace in the ability of democratic regimes to adjust the course as coastlines, reefs, icebergs and sea monsters come into view. But to do so, good analysis and interpretation are needed to avoid bad strategic decisions.

Epilogue

I have chosen to conclude this book with a number of key takeaways – for students of International Relations, for defence analysts, diplomats, strategists, foreign correspondents, risk assessors and, above all, decision makers of all sorts – that derive from this consideration of flawed strategy. One should give others more credit for acting logically on their own values and beliefs, or indeed on their own interpretation of a situation that may be based on factors or information unknown to us or their ignorance of information known to us, which we wrongly assume that they must surely share. As Baroness Neville-Jones put it, one should try to work out 'where they are coming from'.[1] Adversarial governments, we should remember, may be prioritizing factors related to bureaucratic compromises arrived at internally or at the insistence of allies. If they are autocracies like Xi's China or Putin's Russia, confusing and apparently incoherent behaviour may be due to parts of the government or its agents being kept in the dark about what others are doing. If the government structures are looser, different parts may be acting out different agendas, consciously or unconsciously. None of this is a function of being smart or dumb, but of bureaucratic politics.

Epilogue 167

My recommendations below aim to help us guard against our own biases and weaknesses in logic and rationality. They read as follows:

- Avoid talking about 'Ruritania' as though it was a single actor and be alert when anybody else does. Refer to the government, if you don't know any better, but preferably work out who the different actors and forces are and who favours what action within government. Do not affect blindness towards extra-governmental powers, important industrial and other lobbies, even opposition parties.
- Do not try to guess what *you* would do in a particular situation. Try to work out what makes an antagonist (or indeed difficult allies and partners) tick, and what they would think and do in a given situation.
- Do not assume total coherence in any government's decision making and actions. Try to work out, from speeches and statements, which leaders think what. What comes out of the 'black box' of government is unlikely to be coherent, as it will be the product of bureaucratic wrangling to further multiple, often conflicting agendas. Less so in autocracies than in democracies, for sure.
- Be ready to accept that others have values and ideals other than materialism, and are ready to make considerable sacrifices for them. These may be values you cannot relate to.
- Give antagonists more credit for being logical in acting on their values and ideals, however irrational these may seem to you.
- Nevertheless, allow for vanity and the desire to stay in power (which leaders may well justify to themselves as the only way they can protect their higher values and ideals).
- Be conscious of your own biases such as denial, mirror imaging, confirmation bias, . . .
- Beware of thinking that one side's signalling will be interpreted in the way it is intended by the other side in a conflict

168　Epilogue

(or even among allies). Hermetically closed belief systems and systems dominated by conspiracy theories are particularly difficult, or even impossible, to reassure that one's intentions are peaceful.

- Be aware that, while you are assiduously monitoring what you think is important, something else might be much more so. (Or, for my IR colleagues, the question you ask may not get to the heart of what you are trying to study, as an in-depth study would reveal – but the latter should be undertaken without the blinkers of a leading question.)
- Listen to country specialists who are deeply immersed in the culture they study and yet can compare it with others to recognize peculiarities that are significant for issues of war and peace.
- Make a fresh analysis. Better still, get a fresh lot of analysts to reassess a situation at least every 3–5 years or so. Do not get stuck in believing in your own perhaps outdated interpretations when the country or situation you are studying has evolved.
- Do not fall for baseline arguments, statistical probabilities or indeed monocausal explanations when trying to analyse a conflict or a government's strategies and policies.
- Study languages and cultures, go and live in the countries on which you want to be expert, get to understand the traditional views, the historical events that formed the culture, the myths of loss and injustice and national glory and destiny, and see how they might translate into greater ambitions and lessons for war and peace.
- Theories do not replace deep immersion achieved by listening to the arguments of locals (not only the proverbial barbers and taxi drivers), watching television programmes, listening to the radio, and reading, reading, reading. Get guidance on what to read by talking to locals; get into their minds. Look for patterns within particular cultures, not for theoretical explanations with the pretence that one size fits all.

Epilogue

Intelligence pros will already be well acquainted with all or most of these recommendations, and some governments have already drawn extensive lessons from past intelligence failures.[2] These include reports, such as those produced by Nicoll and the Chilcot Inquiry in the United Kingdom or Robert Jervis's report for the CIA,[3] and admirable prescriptions for their own practitioners. One, 'The Good Operation', was produced directly as a result of the Chilcot Inquiry.[4] For smart professionals within government organizations, the recommendations above may nevertheless provide a useful refresher, helping them avoid making bad decisions, resulting in flawed strategies.

Notes

Preface

1 My favourite example is being asked why I didn't set out to 'generate new evidence' (through interviews and opinion polls?!) when I tried to find out whether sixteenth-century military men thought of themselves as living in times of great military-technological transformation.

2 Carl von Clausewitz, *On War*, trans. Peter Paret and Michael Howard (Princeton, NJ: Princeton University Press, 1984), Book I. On a discussion of this methodological approach, see chapter 8, 'What Clausewitz Read', in my *The Strategy Makers: Thoughts on War and Society from Machiavelli to Clausewitz* (Santa Barbara, CA: Praeger-ABC Clio, 2010).

3 See for example my 'Stalin as Hitler's Successor', in Beatrice Heuser and Robert O'Neill (eds), *Securing Peace in Europe, 1945–62* (London: Macmillan, 1992), pp. 17–40.

4 For a discussion of IR theories, see Scott Burchill, Andrew Linklater, Richard Devetak, Jack Donnelly and Terry Nardin (eds), *Theories of International Relations* (5th edn, London: Palgrave, 2013).

5 US Marine Corps War College, *Strategy Primer* (Quantico, VA: Marine Corps University Press, 2021), pp. 101–21. I shall refer to

Notes to pp. ix–6   171

this from time to time to introduce further terms by which such biases are known.

6 David Omand, *How Spies Think: Ten Lessons in Intelligence* (Harmondsworth: Penguin, 2021).

Introduction

1 Jean-Frédéric Morin and Jonathan Paquin, 'How Does Rationality Apply to FPA and What Are Its Limitations?', in *eisdem* (eds), *Foreign Policy Analysis* (London: Palgrave, 2018).

2 Only a few, like Paul Schroeder, have engaged further with them, usually ending up disproving them, thus for example Schroeder in his 'Historical Reality vs Neo-realist Theory', *International Security* 19(1) (1994): 108–48.

3 Historians thus find it bizarre, to say the least, that IR theorists, 2,500 years later, claim to have discovered that 'emotions' play a role in strategy making.

4 Ivan Bloch, *Is War Now Impossible? Being an Abridgement of 'The War of the Future in its Technical, Economic and Political Relations'*, trans. from Russian (London: Grant Richards, 1899), online at https://archive.org/details/iswarnowimpossib00bloc/page/n3/mode/2up?view=theater.

5 Norman Angell, *The Great Illusion: A Study of the Relation of Military Power in Nations to their Economic and Social Advantage* (3rd edn, New York and London: G. P. Putnam's Sons, 1911).

6 Christopher Clarke, *The Sleepwalkers: How Europe Went to War in 1914* (London: Allen Lane, 2012).

7 David M. Valladares, 'Tragedy or Betrayal? Interwar Europe and British Appeasement', *History: Reviews of New Books* 48(2) (2020): 29–32.

8 Following Renwick Monroe with Hill Maher, 'Psychology and Rational Actor Theory', p. 1.

9 Daniel Kahneman, *Thinking, Fast and Slow* (New York: Farrar, Strauss and Giroux, 2011).

10 See, for example, Donald P. Green and Ian Shapiro, *Pathologies*

172   Notes to pp. 6–13

of *Rational Choice Theory* (New Haven, CT: Yale University Press, 1994).

11   Tim Sweijs, *The Use and Utility of Ultimata in Coercive Diplomacy* (London: Palgrave Macmillan, 2023).

12   I concede that much good work has been done to refine our thinking about deterrence and how this can be optimized and tailored towards a particular adversary; see especially Tim Sweijs and Mattia Bertolini, *Dancing in the Dark: The Seven Sins of Deterrence Assessment* (The Hague Centre of Strategic Studies, March 2023).

13   Lawrence Freedman, *Deterrence* (Cambridge: Polity Press, 2004).

14   Lawrence Freedman, 'Israel: Beyond Deterrence' (29 October 2023), https://samf.substack.com/p/israel-beyond-deterrence?utm _source=post-email-title&publication_id=631422&post_id =138371301&utm_campaign=email-post-title&isFreemail=false &r=1tjajs&utm_medium=email.

Chapter 1 The Rational/Irrational Actor Fallacy

1   Herbert Simon, quoted in Kristen Renwick Monroe with Kristen Hill Maher, 'Psychology and Rational Actor Theory', *Political Psychology* 16(1) (March 1995): 3.

2   See, for example, the list in Jon Elster, 'Introduction' in Jon Elster (ed.), *Rational Choice* (New York: New York University Press, 1986), p. 4; and Renwick Monroe and Hill Maher, 'Psychology and Rational Actor Theory', p. 2.

3   William Riker, 'The Political Psychology of Rational Choice Theory', *Political Psychology* 16(1) (March 1995): 37.

4   Renwick Monroe and Hill Maher, 'Psychology and Rational Actor Theory', p. 6.

5   Roxanne Euben, 'When Worldviews Collide: Conflicting Assumptions about Human Behavior Held by Rational Actor Theory and Islamic Fundamentalism', *Political Psychology* 16(1) (March 1995): 169–73. See also Robert Nalbandov, 'Irrational Rationality of Terrorism', *Journal of Strategic Studies* 6(4) (Winter 2013): 92–102.

Notes to pp. 14–27

6 Quoted in Heinrich August Winkler, *Der Lange Weg nach Westen: Deutsche Geschichte vom "Dritten Reich" bis zur Wiedervereinigung* (Munich: Beck, 2000), p. 4.

7 John Mearsheimer and Sebastian Rosato, *How States Think: The Rationality of Foreign Policy* (New Haven, CT: Yale University Press, 2023).

8 This is to be kept in mind when arguing about the possibility of nuclear war: it is alleged that Israel would have a 'Samson strategy' of bringing down its enemies along with itself rather than incurring the risk of another holocaust.

9 Beatrice Heuser, *Nuclear Mentalities? Strategies and Beliefs in Britain, France and the FRG* (London: Macmillan, 1998).

10 Frederick Russell, *The Just War in the Middle Ages* (Cambridge: Cambridge University Press, 1975), p. 217f.

11 Julian Chrysostomides, 'Byzantine Views on Warfare', in Anja V. Hartmann and Beatrice Heuser (eds), *War, Peace and World Orders from Antiquity until the Twentieth Century* (London: Routledge, 2001), pp. 85–90.

12 Isabelle Duyvesteyn and Beatrice Heuser, 'Grand Patterns of Strategy, Old and New', in Jeremy Black (ed.), *The Practice of Strategy: A Global History* (Società Italiana di Storia Militare: Nadir Media Srl, 2024), pp. 19–36.

13 Oddly, after decades of fighting Islamists, there is much convergence between these Russian 'traditional values' and those of conservative Muslims. One wonders when Putin and Lavrov will start building on this realization in their grand strategy.

14 Beatrice Heuser, 'NSC 68 and the Soviet Threat: A New Perspective on Western Threat Perception and Policy Making', *Review of International Studies* 17(1) (January 1991): 17–40.

15 Beatrice Heuser, *Western Containment Policies in the Cold War: The Yugoslav Case, 1948–1953* (London & New York: Routledge, 1989).

16 Ibid.

17 Full text in https://www.digitalhistory.uh.edu/disp_textbook .cfm?smtID=3&psid=3631.

174   Notes to pp. 27–38

18 Jonathan Corrado, 'Rethinking Intelligence Failure: China's Intervention in the Korean War', *International Journal of Intelligence and CounterIntelligence* 36(1) (2023): 199–219.

19 Shen Zhihua, *Mao, Stalin, and the Korean War: Trilateral Communist Relations in the 1950s*, trans. Neil Silver (London: Routledge, 2012).

20 Graham Allison, *Essence of Decision: Explaining the Cuban Missile Crisis* (Boston, MA: Little, Brown, 1971).

21 James Scott, *Deciding to Intervene: The Reagan Doctrine and American Foreign Policy* (Durham, NC: Duke University Press, 1996).

22 Allison, *Essence of Decision*.

23 For example, see Kevin Marsh, 'Obama's Surge: A Bureaucratic Politics Analysis of the Decision to Order a Troop Surge in the Afghanistan War', *Foreign Policy Analysis* 10(3) (2014): 265–88.

24 For example, when representatives of their states at NATO are waiting for instructions from their capitals on how to decide in internal NATO negotiations, this is referred to as 'nations are deliberating'. What is meant is that some parts of the *governments* of the member states are actively considering proposals, not that there are public debates among or even referenda held by the nations of the member-states.

25 In the sense of tasks, areas within their purview of decision making.

26 Zara Steiner, 'Decision-making in American and British Foreign Policy: An Open and Shut Case', *Review of International Studies* 13(1) (1987): 1–18.

27 Rainer Marcowitz, 'The Yalta Myth', in Cyril Buffet and Beatrice Heuser (eds), *Haunted by History* (Oxford: Berghahn, 1998), pp. 80–91.

28 The document itself – a scrap of paper – can be seen at http:// cassidyglobalcoldwar.weebly.com/percentage-deal.html.

29 See also Richard Ned Lebow, 'Windows of Opportunity: Do States Jump through Them?' *International Security* 9(1) (1984): 147–86.

Notes to pp. 39–45

30 There is a French lore that in the Franco-Prussian War of 1870–1, German troops stole clocks from French houses; to prevent worse looting, when the Germans invaded again in 1914, the French put their grandfather clocks outside their doors in the hope that the Germans would just take these and leave the rest alone. By then, however, grandfather clocks had made it to German households as well, so the trick did not work.

31 Anthony Beevor, *Arnhem: The Battle for the Bridges, 1944* (London: Viking, 2018).

32 Rodric Braithwaite, *Afgantsy: The Russians in Afghanistan, 1979–1989* (Oxford: Oxford University Press, 2011), p. 57.

33 This reads:

> The Parties agree that an armed attack against one or more of them in Europe or North America shall be considered an attack against them all and consequently they agree that, if such an armed attack occurs, each of them, in exercise of the right of individual or collective self-defence recognized by Article 51 of the Charter of the United Nations, will assist the Party or Parties so attacked by taking forthwith, individually and in concert with the other Parties, such action as it deems necessary, including the use of armed force, to restore and maintain the security of the North Atlantic area.

34 In late 1995, only a few months after the Srebrenica massacre, the United States, with the support of other states, managed to impose a peace agreement on the warring factions of Bosnia-Herzegovina, underpinned by the deployment of an Implementation Force (IFOR), which after a year got a new mandate and name as a Security Force (SFOR) under the command of NATO.

35 Robert Anthony Pape, *Bombing to Win: Air Power and Coercion in War* (Ithaca, NY: Cornell University Press, 1996).

36 There were also many allegations at the time that historical alignments between France and Serbia (and thus the Yugoslav government) and Germany and Croatia supposedly influenced

176 Notes to pp. 47–50

policy making in the earlier 1990s. Contemporary concerns played a much greater part, however: Germany's support for self-determination was the logical corollary to Germany's reunification through self-determination, which Hans-Dietrich Genscher, the extremely influential German minister of foreign affairs, underscored unrelentingly; French President François Mitterrand's reluctance to support Yugoslavia's disintegration was in turn connected with his fear of Breton and Corsican independence movements in a period of reborn nationalist-secessionist sentiments, of which the Yugoslav Wars were only the most drastic example.

37 Zana Tofiq Kaka Amin, 'Why Did the United States Lead an Invasion of Iraq in 2003?', *International Journal of Political Science and Development* 2(11) (2014): 301–8.

38 Robert Jervis, *Why Intelligence Fails* (Ithaca, NY: Cornell University Press, 2010), pp. 123–55, here p. 136. On Curveball, see Bob Drogin, *Curveball: Spies, Lies and the Man Behind Them: The Real Reason America Went to War in Iraq* (New York: Random House, 2008).

39 Jervis, *Why Intelligence Fails*, pp. 123–55. On 'Curveball', see Drogin, *Curveball*.

40 https://www.iraqbodycount.org/.

41 Steve Yetiv, *The Absence of Grand Strategy: The United States in the Persian Gulf, 1972–2005* (Johns Hopkins University Press, 2008).

42 Robert Jervis, 'Why Nuclear Superiority Doesn't Matter', *Political Science Quarterly* 94(4) (Winter 1979–1980), p. 621f.

43 Hans Morgenthau, 'The Four Paradoxes of Nuclear Strategy', *American Political Science Review* 58(1) (1964): 25.

44 Thomas C. Schelling, *The Strategy of Conflict* (Cambridge, MA: Harvard University Press, 1960), ch. 8.

45 Roger Morgan, 'Saving Face for the Sake of Deterrence', in Robert Jervis, Richard Ned Lebow and Janice Gross Stein, *Psychology and Deterrence* (Washington, DC: Johns Hopkins University Press, 1985), pp. 128, 131.

Notes to pp. 51–8

46 See section below, 'Driven by a different agenda'.
47 https://www.youtube.com/watch?v=_SsccRkLLzU.

Chapter 2 Our Biases

1 Quoted in Robert Jervis, *Why Intelligence Fails* (Ithaca, NY: Cornell University Press, 2010), p. 176f.
2 Catherine Grace Katz, *The Daughters of Yalta: The Churchills, Roosevelts, and Harriman: A Story of Love and War* (Boston: Houghton Mifflin Harcourt, 2020), pp. 145–6.
3 For the full text of Hitler's directive of 18 December 1941, see https://de.wikisource.org/wiki/Fall_Barbarossa.
4 Ian Kershaw, *Fateful Choices: Ten Decisions that Changed the World, 1940–1941* (London: Allen Lane, 2007).
5 Quoted in Jervis, *Why Intelligence Fails*, p. 177.
6 Nicoll Report ('The JIC, and Warning of Aggression'), November 1981, excerpts printed in Robert Dover and Michael Goodman (eds), *Learning from the Secret Past: Cases from British Intelligence History* (Washington, DC: Georgetown University Press, 2011), pp. 277–92, here p. 279.
7 The transcript is available at https://msuweb.montclair.edu/~furrg/glaspie.html.
8 Robert Jervis, 'Introduction: Approach and Assumptions', in Robert Jervis et al., *Psychology and Deterrence* (Washington, DC: Johns Hopkins University Press, 1985), p. 1.
9 Frank Pringle, 'A Fraught Subordination: Analysing the Relationship between the Soviet Union and East Germany during the "Second Cold War", 1979–1984', MS, MSc dissertation, University of Glasgow, 2024.
10 Beatrice Heuser, 'Military Exercises and the Dangers of Misunderstandings: The East–West Crisis of the early 1980s', in Beatrice Heuser, Tormod Heier and Guillaume Lasconjarias (eds), *Military Exercises: Political Messaging and Strategic Impact*, Forum Paper 26 (Rome: NATO Defence College, 2018), http://www.ndc.nato.int/download/downloads.php?icode=546.
11 Ibid.; see also Beatrice Heuser, 'The Soviet Response to the

178   Notes to pp. 59–64

Euromissile Crisis, 1982–83', in Leopoldo Nuti (ed.), *The Crisis of Détente in Europe: From Helsinki to Gorbachev, 1975–1985* (London: Routledge, 2008), pp. 137–49.

12 Jonathan Riley-Smith, *What Were the Crusades?* (4th edn, London: Bloomsbury, 2009).

13 We have confirmation of this in Muslim sources; see Sadr al-Din al-Husayni, *Akhbar al-dawla al-saljuqiyya* (*c.* early mid-thirteenth century), trans. Clifford Edmund Bosworth, *The History of the Seljuk State* (Abingdon: Routledge, 2011), p. 37f.; and sources quoted in Niall Christie, 'Religious Campaign or War of Conquest? Muslim Views of the Motives of the First Crusade', in Niall Christie and Maya Yazigi (eds), *Noble Ideals and Bloody Reality* (Leiden: Brill, 2006), p. 59.

14 Pope Urban's appeal was recorded i.a. by Robert the Monk *c.* 25 years later, text in Dana C. Munro, 'Urban and the Crusaders', *Translations and Reprints from the Original Sources of European History* 1(2) (Philadelphia: University of Pennsylvania, 1895), pp. 5–8.

15 Jonathan Riley-Smith, 'Crusading as an Act of Love', *History* 65(214) (1980): 177–92.

16 Michael Mitterauer, 'The Crusades and Protocolonialism: The Roots of European Expansionism', in Mitterauer, *Why Europe? The Medieval Origins of its Special Path*, trans. Gerald Chapple (Chicago, IL: University of Chicago Press, 2010), pp. 194–231.

17 Michael Kandiah (ed.), *The Role and Function of the British Embassy in Beijing* in the Witness Seminar Series (London: Foreign and Commonwealth Office and King's College London, 2012), pp. 41–4, 52, 54, https://issuu.com/fcohistorians/docs/beijing_embassy_witness_seminar_tra.

18 Ibid., p. 43.

19 Jervis, *Why Intelligence Fails*, p. 25.

20 Nicoll Report, in Dover and Goodman (eds), *Learning from the Secret Past*, p. 279.

21 Research carried out by Friedrich Ebert Foundation's 'Security

Notes to pp. 64–72

Radar' in 2019, see http://library.fes.de/pdf-files/bueros/wien/15 176-20190412.pdf.

22 https://library.fes.de/pdf-files/bueros/wien/18980-20220310.pdf.

23 http://library.fes.de/pdf-files/bueros/wien/15176-20190412.pdf.

24 https://library.fes.de/pdf-files/bueros/wien/18980-20220310.pdf.

25 https://www.levada.ru/en/ The FES polls of late 2021 show 57 per cent hostility to the United States.

26 http://library.fes.de/pdf-files/bueros/wien/15176-20190412.pdf.

27 Robert Jervis, *Perception and Misperception in International Politics* (Princeton, NJ: Princeton University Press, 1976), p. 152.

28 Dimitri Minic, *Pensée et culture stratégiques russes* (Paris: Maison des Sciences de l'Homme, 2023), ch. 5 ; Dima Adamsky, *The Russian Way of Deterrence: Strategic Culture, Coercion, and War* (Stanford, CA: Stanford University Press, 2024).

29 Edward Luttwak, 'Why We Need More Waste, Fraud and Mismanagement in the Pentagon,' *Survival* 24(3) (1982): 117–30.

30 Report of the Iraq Enquiry, https://webarchive.nationalarchives .gov.uk/ukgwa/20171123122743/http://www.iraqinquiry.org.uk /the-report/.

31 The transcript is available at https://msuweb.montclair.edu/~ furrg/glaspie.html.

32 Nicoll Report, in Dover and Goodman (eds), *Learning from the Secret Past*, pp. 277–92.

33 Nicoll Report, in Dover and Goodman (eds), *Learning from the Secret Past*, p. 280.

34 Amnon Sofrin, 'The Intelligence Failure of October 7 – Roots and Lessons', *Jerusalem Strategic Tribune* (26 November 2023), https://jstribune.com/sofrim-the-intelligence-failure-of-october -7-roots-and-lessons/.

35 https://www.arte.tv/de/videos/115611-004-A/prigoschins-tod -im-kreml-tv/. Her series of analyses on the Russian media is a must-follow for any media student and can be found on ARTE, the Franco-German channel – do not confuse with Russia Today, cleverly abbreviated as 'RT' which sounds the same.

36 Ibid.

180   Notes to pp. 73–81

37 Michael Herman pioneered academic writing by ex-British intelligence officers; see his *Intelligence Power in Peace and War* (Cambridge: Cambridge University Press for the Royal Institute of International Affairs, 1996).

38 Christopher Andrew and Oleg Gordievsky, *Instructions from the Centre: Top Secret Files on KGB Foreign Operations, 1975–85* (London: Hodder & Stoughton, 1993); Jordan Baev, 'War Scare Psychosis and Operation VRYaN: New Evidence from Bulgarian Military and Intelligence Archives', in Hans-Peter Kriemann and Matej Medvecky (eds), *From Peace to War, from War to Peace* (Potsdam: ZMS Bw, 2024), p. 153.

39 Rebecca Harding and Jack Harding, *Gaming Trade: Win–Win Strategies for the Digital Era* (London: London Publishing Partnership, 2019).

40 https://www.youtube.com/watch?v=IGQmdoK_ZfY.

41 Sir Arthur Conan Doyle, *The Adventure of Silver Blaze* (Paisley: Gleniffer Press, s.d.).

42 For example, Gen. A. V. Seryhantov, Gen. A. V. Smolovy, Col. A. V. Dolgopolov, 'Transformation of the Concept of War from Past to Present: Hybrid Warfare Technologies', trans. from Russian, *Military Review* (Moscow) 30(1) (2021); see also 'The Concept of the Foreign Policy of the Russian Federation', Decree of the President of the Russian Federation No. 229 (31 March 2023), Para. 49.1.

43 Michael Plötz and Hans-Peter Müller, *Ferngelenkte Friedensbewegung? DDR und UdSSR im Kampf gegen den NATO Doppelbeschluss* (Münster: LIT Verlag, 2004).

44 Beatrice Heuser, 'The Soviet Response to the Euromissile Crisis, 1982–83', in Leopoldo Nuti (ed.), *The Crisis of Détente in Europe: From Helsinki to Gorbachev, 1975–1985* (London: Routledge, 2008), pp. 137–49.

45 http://www.mirror.co.uk/news/uk-news/beautiful-young-woman-killed-cervical-4782612.

46 Rolf Dobelli, *The Art of Thinking Clearly*, trans. Nicky Griffin (New York: HarperCollins, 2013), p. 164.

Notes to pp. 81–91

47 Jervis, 'Introduction', p. 10f.

48 Comment by Paul Schulte in a note to the author, 24 August 2023.

49 https://www.lefigaro.fr/nice/disparition-d-emile-il-y-a-des-affa ires-qu-on-sait-criminelles-mais-sans-qu-aucune-piste-n-emer ge-20230729.

50 Milovan Djilas, *Conversations with Stalin*, trans. Michael Petrovich (London: Rupert Hart-Davis, 1962), p. 164.

51 Beatrice Heuser, 'Stalin as Hitler's Successor', in Beatrice Heuser and Robert O'Neill (eds), *Securing Peace in Europe, 1945–62* (London: Macmillan, 1992), pp. 17–40.

52 See https://twitter.com/fahrettinaltun/status/129797122359135 8465.

53 Ofer Fridman, 'From "Putin the Saviour" to "Irreplaceable Putin": The Role of the 1990s in the Kremlin's Strategic Communications', *Defence Strategic Communications* 10 (Spring–Autumn 2021): 153–95.

54 'The Putin Files', interviews with Kara Murza (2016), https:// www.youtube.com/watch?v=yIibXQU_dgo.

55 Jervis, *Why Intelligence Fails*, p. 138.

56 Uri Bar Joseph, *The Angel: The Egyptian Spy Who Saved Israel* (New York: Harper, repr. 2017).

57 Nicoll Report, in Dover and Goodman (eds), *Learning from the Secret Past*, p. 282.

58 Béla K. Király, 'The Hungarian Revolution and the Soviet Readiness to Wage War against Socialist States', in Béla K. Király, Barbara Lotze and Nandor Dreisziger (eds), *The First War Between Socialist States: The Hungarian Revolution of 1956 and its Impact* (New York: Brooklyn College Press, distributed by Columbia University Press, 1984).

59 Dover and Goodman (eds), *Learning from the Secret Past*, p. 292.

60 John Gill, 'India, Pakistan and Brasstacks: Exercise and Crisis on the Edge of War', in Beatrice Heuser, Tormod Heier, Guillaume Lasconjarias and Denis Mercier (eds), *Military Exercises,*

182 Notes to pp. 94–103

http://www.ndc.nato.int/download/downloads.php?icode=546, pp. 302–32.

61 Quoted in Minic, *Pensée et culture stratégiques russes*, p. 339.

62 Florence Gaub, *Zukunft: Eine Bedienungsanleitung* (Munich: dtv, 2023), p. 126f.

63 David Omand, *How Spies Think: Ten Lessons in Intelligence* (Harmondsworth: Penguin, 2021), p. 72f.

64 Albert Speer, *Inside the Third Reich*, trans. Richard and Clara Winston (London: Weidenfeld & Nicolson, 1970), p. 346.

65 Bogdan Musial, *Sowjetische Partisanen 1941–1944: Mythos und Wirklichkeit* (Paderborn: Ferdinand Schöningh, 2009), p. 36; Alexander Hill (ed.), *The Great Patriotic War of the Soviet Union 1941–1945: A Documentary Reader* (London: Routledge, 2009), p. 193.

66 Roberta Wohlstetter, *Pearl Harbor: Warning and Decision* (Stanford, CA: Stanford University Press, 1962).

67 David S. Yost, 'Political Philosophy and the Theory of International Relations', *International Affairs* 70(2) (April 1994): 285.

68 Vladimir Putin, '50 Years of the European integration and Russia', *Sunday Times* (25 March 2007).

69 Robert Petersen, 'Fear and Loathing in Moscow: The Russian Biological Weapons Programme in 2022', *Bulletin of the Atomic Scientists* (5 October 2022), https://thebulletin.org/2022/10/the -russian-biological-weapons-program-in-2022/#post-heading

70 Alternative Defence Commission, *Defence without the Bomb* (London: Taylor and Francis, 1983), and id., *Without the Bomb* (London: Paladin & Granada, 1985).

71 US National Security Strategy of 2022, https://www.whiteh ouse.gov/wp-content/uploads/2022/11/8-November-Combined -PDF-for-Upload.pdf.

72 Wohlstetter, *Pearl Harbor*, p. 167f.

73 Marja Nykänen, 'Black Swans and Grey Rhinos – Lessons of Crises on Macroprudential Policy', Conference on Systemic Risk Analytics, Helsinki, 5 May 2022, https://www.bis.org/review/r22 0509c.htm.

Notes to pp. 104–13

74 https://www.9-11commission.gov/report/911Report.pdf, p. 260f.
75 John Kiszely, *Anatomy of a Campaign: The British Fiasco in Norway, 1940* (Cambridge: Cambridge University Press, 2019).
76 House of Commons Defence Committee, 'Withdrawal from Afghanistan', Fifth Report of Session 2022–23 (1 February 2023), https://committees.parliament.uk/publications/33946/documents/186082/default/.
77 Victor Davis Hanson, *The Western Way of War: Infantry Battle in Classical Greece* (New York: Alfred Knopf, 1989).
78 All examples discussed by Dominic Johnson, *Overconfidence and War* (Boston, MA: Harvard University Press, 2004).

Chapter 3 Knowns and Unknowns (and How We Use Them)
1 Daniel Kahneman, *Thinking, Fast and Slow* (New York: Farrar, Strauss and Giroux, 2011), pp. 85–90.
2 Quoted in Robert Jervis, *Why Intelligence Fails* (Ithaca, NY: Cornell University Press, 2010), p. 156.
3 Miles Kahler, 'Rationality in International Relations', *Political Psychology* 16(1) (March 1995): 926.
4 Rolf Dobelli, *The Art of Thinking Clearly*, trans. Nicky Griffin (New York: HarperCollins, 2013), p. 176.
5 Jean-Jacques Rousseau, 'An Inquiry into the Nature of the Social Contract; or Principles of Political Right' (Dublin: B. Smith for William Jones, 1712); Oswald Spengler, *Der Untergang des Abendlandes* (Vienna: Braunmüller, 1918); Aleksandr Dugin, *The Foundations of Geopolitics: The Geopolitical Future of Russia* (orig. in Russian, Moscow: Arktogeya, 1997).
6 A great example of this is Lion Feuchtwanger's novel *The Oppermanns*, written in France in 1934 (!) after he had fled the first wave of Nazi persecutions and internments in concentration camps of 1933–4, a prophecy of the Holocaust ignored by so many Jews at their peril until it was too late.
7 'Falkland Islands Review' of January 1983, aka Franks Report, https://c59574e9047e61130f13-3f71d0fe2b653c4f00f32175760e

184 Notes to pp. 114–21

96e7.ssl.cf1.rackcdn.com/E415E0802DAA482297D889B9B43B7 0DE.pdf, paras 129–33.

8 Ibid. (Franks Report), paras 316 and 317.

9 Kevin McCall, 'Lee's Blind Horses', in Christian B. Keller (ed.), *Southern Strategies: Why the Confederacy Failed* (Kansas, MO: University Press of Kansas, 2021), pp. 101–8.

10 D. C. Watt, *How War Came* (London: Heinemann, 1989), pp. 101f, 137.

11 Irving Janis, *Victims of Groupthink: A Psychological Study of Foreign-Policy Decisions and Fiascoes* (Boston: Houghton Mifflin, 1972).

12 Colin Elman and Miriam Elman, 'Introduction', *eisdem* (eds), *Bridges and Boundaries: Historians, Political Scientists and the Study of International Relations* (Boston: MIT Press, 2000), p. 7.

13 Quoted ibid., p. 14.

14 Bertrand Russell, 'On Induction', *The Problems of Philosophy* (Home University Library, 1912), ch. VI.

15 Nasim Nicholas Taleb, *The Black Swan; or The Impact of the Highly Improbable* (London: Random House, 2010), p. 40.

16 Bruno Tertrais, '"On the Brink" – Really? Revisiting Nuclear Close Calls since 1945', *Washington Quarterly* 40(2) (2017): 51–6.

17 Benoît Pelopidas, 'The Unbearable Lightness of Luck: Three Sources of Overconfidence in the Manageability of Nuclear Crises', *European Journal of International Security* 2(2) (2017): 240–62.

18 This was the reasoning underlying Soviet doctrine and exercises for the use of nuclear weapons in the second half of the Cold War; see Beatrice Heuser, 'Warsaw Pact Military Doctrines in the 70s and 80s: Findings in the East German Archives', *Comparative Strategy* 12(4) (Oct.–Dec. 1993): 437–57; and Beatrice Heuser, 'Victory in a Nuclear War? A Comparison of NATO and WTO War Aims and Strategies', *Contemporary European History* 7(3) (November 1998): 311–28.

19 Possible wild cards and their consequences are deliberately identified in foresight work done within defence ministries.

20 Dobelli, *Art of Thinking Clearly*, p. 290.

21 Nasim Nicholas Taleb, *Fooled by Randomness: The Hidden Role of Chance in Life and in the Markets* (Harmondsworth: Penguin, 2007).

22 Thucydides 1.23.5–10.

23 For a discussion of the previous crises, see Christopher Clark, *The Sleepwalkers* (London: Allen Lane, 2012).

24 Beatrice Heuser, 'Fortuna, Chance, Risk and Opportunity in Strategy', *Journal of Strategic Studies* 45(5) (2022): 1–26.

25 Clausewitz, *On War*, I.1.28.

26 Quoted in Bruno Colson, *Napoléon: De la guerre* (Paris: Perrin, 2011), p. 54.

27 See, for example, John Baylis, Steven Smith and Patricia Owens, 'Introduction', in *eisdem* (eds), *The Globalisation of World Politics: An Introduction to International Relations* (9th edn, Oxford: Oxford University Press, 2022).

28 Anne-Sofie Dahl, 'The Myth of Swedish Neutrality', in Cyril Buffet and Beatrice Heuser (eds), *Haunted by History* (Oxford: Berghahn, 1998), pp. 28–40; Robert Dalsjö, *Life-Line Lost: The Rise and Fall of 'Neutral' Sweden's Secret Reserve Option of Wartime Help from the West* (Stockholm: Sanderus Press, 2006).

29 Longer-term strategy for the North Atlantic Treaty Organization in its International Security Assistance Force role in Afghanistan, approved by the North Atlantic Council on 1 October 2003 and submitted by Lord Robertson, the NATO secretary general, to Kofi Annan, the UN secretary-general, on 2 October 2003, available in UN Security Council document 2/2003/970. I owe this reference to Professor David Yost.

30 Beatrice Heuser, 'The World in Transition, and What the Biden Administration Tries to Do About It', in Michaela Dodge and Matthew R. Costlow (eds), *Expert Commentary on the 2022 National Security Strategy* (Fairfax, VA: National Institute Press, 2022), pp. 57–68, https://nipp.org/wp-content/uploads/2023/01/OP-Vol-3-No.-2.pdf.

31 Examples include the communists in French President

186   Notes to pp. 132–9

Mitterrand's first government of 1981–1984, and the Green
Party in Germany's government of 2021.

Chapter 4 Flaws and Quandaries of Strategy Making

1 See Nathan Leite's *Study of Bolshevism* (Glencoe, IL: The Free
Press, 1953); and Alexander George's discussion thereof in 'The
"Operational Code": A Neglected Approach to the Study of
Political Leaders and Decision-Making', *International Studies
Quarterly* 13(2) (June 1969): 190–222.

2 Beatrice Heuser, 'Covert Action within British and American
Concepts of "Containment"', in Richard Aldrich (ed.), *British
Intelligence, Strategy and the Cold War, 1945–51* (London:
Routledge, 1992), pp. 65–84.

3 George Crile, *Charlie Wilson's War: The Extraordinary Story
of the Largest Covert Operation in History* (New York: Atlantic
Monthly Press, 2003).

4 Ian Kershaw, *The 'Hitler Myth': Image and Reality in the Third
Reich* (Oxford: Oxford University Press, 1987).

5 Markus Wolf with Anne McElvoy, *Man without a Face: The
Autobiography of Communism's Greatest Spymaster* (London:
Jonathan Cape, 1997).

6 https://www.linkedin.com/in/steven-m-3785ba/?originalSubdo
main=uk.

7 Steven R. Mann, 'Chaos Theory and Strategic Thought',
Parameters (Autumn 1992): 54–8.

8 Dimitri Minic, *Pensée et culture stratégiques russes* (Paris: Maison
des Sciences de l'Homme, 2023), pp. 323–9.

9 These go back to Henry David Thoreau and Gene Sharp, *On the
Duty of Civil Disobedience* (Peace News Pamphlet, 1963).

10 Minic, *Pensée et culture stratégiques russes*, pp. 311–26
passim.

11 Edward Luttwak, *The Rise of China vs the Logic of Strategy*
(Cambridge, MA: Harvard University Press, 2012), ch. 2.

12 Anon. [Guibert], *General Essay de Tactique* (London: chez les
libraires associés, 1772), repr. in Comte de Guibert, *Stratégiques*,

with an introduction by Jean-Paul Charnay (Paris: Herne, 1977), my translation.

13 [Otto August] R[ühle] von L[ilienstern], 'Apologie des Krieges', in idem, *Aufsätze über Gegenstände und Ereignisse aus dem Gebiete des Kriegswesens* (Berlin: Ernst Siegfried Mittler, 1818), p. 187 (my translation).

14 On timelines, see also Andrew Carr, 'It's about Time: Strategy and Temporal Phenomena', *Journal of Strategic Studies* 44(3) (2021): 303–24.

15 Gjert Lage Dyndal and Peer Hilde, 'Strategic Thinking in NATO and the "New Military Strategy" of 2019', in Janne Haaland Matlary and Rob Johnson (eds), *Military Strategy in the 21st Century* (London: Hurst, 2020), pp. 225–32.

16 Peter Ricketts, *Hard Choices: The Making and Unmaking of Global Britain* (New York: Atlantic Books, 2022).

17 On ultimata, see Tim Sweijs, *The Use and Utility of Ultimata in Coercive Diplomacy* (Basingstoke: Palgrave Macmillan, 2023), here esp. ch. 1.

18 David Omand, *How Spies Think: Ten Lessons in Intelligence* (Harmondsworth: Penguin, 2021), p. 124.

19 Kahneman, *Thinking, Fast and Slow*; Dobelli, *Art of Thinking Clearly*.

20 As an eyewitness recalled, Spaak, back in his rooms, cracked open a fresh bottle of champagne, went out onto his balcony and intoned 'O Sole Mio'. Pinay, who unbeknownst to him occupied the suite above him, shouted down, 'Stop it, Spaak, you've tormented me all last night. At least now give me a little sleep.'

21 I am grateful to Samuël Kruizinga for having brought this story to my attention. See https://www.ewmagazine.nl/buitenland/news/2014/04/hoe-oud-minister-wim-beyen-op-sicili-de-basis-voor-de-eu-legde-1504762W/.

22 United Kingdom Parliament Defence Committee Report, 'Withdrawal from Afghanistan', Fifth Report of Session 2022–2023 (10 Feb. 2023); Deutscher Bundestag, 'Zwischenbericht der Enquete-Kommission Lehren aus Afghanistan für das künftige

188 Notes to pp. 147–63

vernetzte Engagement Deutschlands', Drucksache 20/10400 (19 February 2024).

23 Dobelli, *Art of Thinking Clearly*, p. 54.

24 Michael Hastings, *The Operators: The Wild and Terrifying Inside Story of America's War in Afghanistan* (Boston, MA: Blue Rider Press, 2012).

25 De Gaulle's announcement of nuclear cooperation with the USSR was made in October 1966, see 'De Gaulle to Give Press Conference', *Times* (13 Oct. 1966).

26 This was told at an Oral History session of the Nuclear History Program, Institut de France, in 1990, transcripts now at the Archives des Services Historiques des Armées, Château de Vincennes.

27 The texts of successive communiqués can be found at https://www.dfi.de/dossiers/deutsch-franzoesische-gipfel.

28 Kenton White, *Never Ready: Britain's Armed Forces and NATO's Flexible Response Strategy, 1967–1989* (Warwick: Helion, 2022).

29 Dobelli, *Art of Thinking Clearly*, p. 203.

30 Sir Lawrence Freedman, *Official History of the Falklands Campaign*, Vol. 1, *The Origins of the Falklands War* (London: Routledge, 2005), esp. pp. 46–54, 66–75, 132f.

31 Freedman, *Official History* 1: 140–58.

32 'Falkland Islands Review' of January 1983, aka Franks Report, https://c59574e9047e61130f13-3f71d0fe2b653c4f00f32175760e96e7.ssl.cf1.rackcdn.com/E415E0802DAA482297D889B9B43B70DE.pdf, paras 280, 283.

33 Steve Yetiv, *National Security through a Cockeyed Lens: How Cognitive Bias Impacts US Foreign Policy* (Baltimore, MD: Johns Hopkins University Press, 2013), ch. 2.

34 Stig Förster, 'Dreams and Nightmares: German Military Leadership and the Images of Future Warfare, 1871–1914', in Manfred Boemeke, Roger Chickering and Stig Förster (eds), *Anticipating Total War: The German and American Experiences, 1871–1914* (Cambridge: CUP, 1999), pp. 343–76.

35 Lawrence Freedman, *Strategy: A History* (Oxford: Oxford University Press, 2012), pp. 589–97.

Epilogue

1 RUSI Talking Strategy Podcasts, Season 4, https://www.rusi.org/podcast-series/talking-strategy-podcast.
2 Sir David Omand has done an exceptionally good job of formulating similar admonitions for intelligence agencies and analysts; and excellent advice for strategy and policy *makers* is also included in Steve Yetiv's *National Security through a Cockeyed Lens*; see Bibliography.
3 Robert Jervis, *Why Intelligence Fails* (Ithaca, NY: Cornell University Press, 2010).
4 In the United Kingdom, the Ministry of Defence's *Good Operation*, https://www.gov.uk/government/publications/the-good-operation; and the Foreign, Commonwealth and Development Office's *Programme Operating Framework*, https://www.gov.uk/government/publications/fcdo-programme-operating-framework.

Select Bibliography

Dover, Robert and Goodman, Michael (eds), 2011. *Learning from the Secret Past: Cases in British Intelligence History* (Washington, DC: Georgetown University Press), chs by Gill Bennet on Suez, Len Scott on the Cuban Missile Crisis, Michael Goodman on the Nicoll Report on the avoidance of surprises.

Jervis, Robert, 1976. *Perception and Misperception in International Politics* (Princeton, NJ: Princeton University Press).

Jervis, Robert, 2010. *Why Intelligence Fails* (Ithaca, NY: Cornell University Press).

Jervis, Robert, Lebow, Richard Ned and Stein, Janice Gross, 1985. *Psychology and Deterrence* (Washington, DC: Johns Hopkins University Press).

Kahneman, Daniel, 2012. *Thinking, Fast and Slow* (Harmondsworth: Penguin).

Keegan, John, 2004. *Intelligence in War: Knowledge of the Enemy from Napoleon to Al Qaeda* (London: Pimlico).

Lynn, Jonathan and Jay, Anthony, 1989. *The Complete Yes Minister* (London: BBC Books).

Omand, David, 2021. *How Spies Think: Ten Lessons in Intelligence* (Harmondsworth: Penguin).

Scott, James, 1996. *Deciding to Intervene: The Reagan Doctrine*

Select Bibliography

and American Foreign Policy (Durham, NC: Duke University Press).

UK Ministry of Defence, 2018. *Good Operation*, https://www.gov.uk/government/publications/the-good-operation.

Yetiv, Steve, 2013. *National Security Through a Cockeyed Lens: How Cognitive Bias Impacts US Foreign Policy* (Baltimore, MD: Johns Hopkins University Press).